VE THAT DROP THE
N TV KIDS
GLOBAL WARMING
COOK WOW
DS A MEAL
WHAT IS A KID'S MEAL
CONSERVE
USE ORGANIC
ONAL WHAT FOOTPRINT
SLOW DOWN
SLOW FOOD
GLOBAL FINANCIAL CRISIS
DE HEALTH
EAPEST
WHAT IS VALUE?
NT HIGH FAT
LESS FUTURE LOW FAT
GENERATIONS
FOOD STOP

THE URBAN COOK

MARK JENSEN

COOKING AND EATING FOR A SUSTAINABLE FUTURE

MURDOCH BOOKS

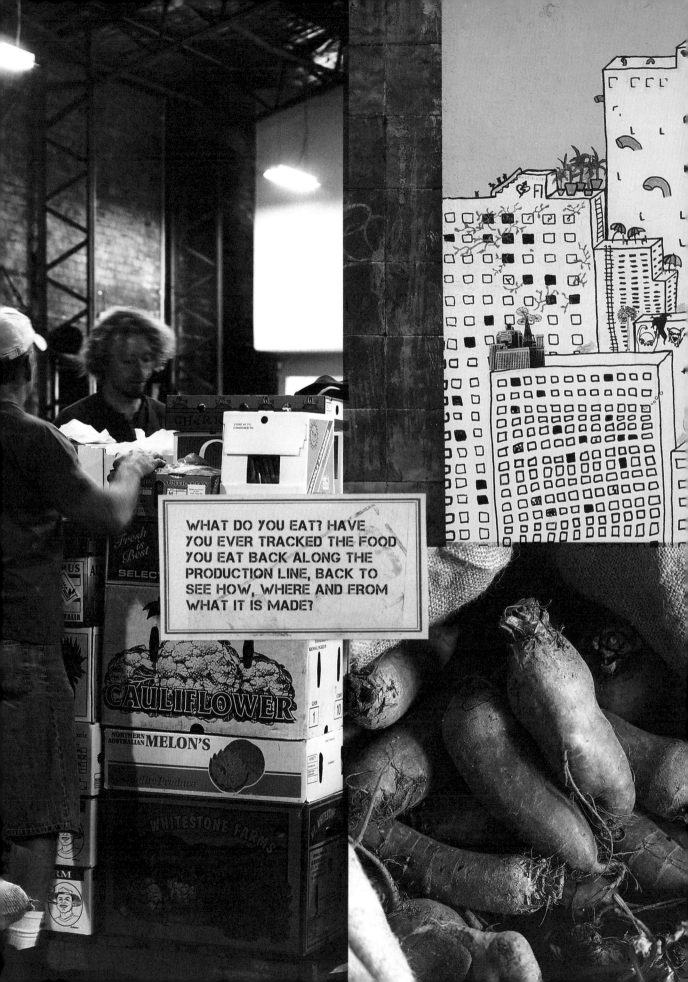

WHAT DO YOU EAT? HAVE YOU EVER TRACKED THE FOOD YOU EAT BACK ALONG THE PRODUCTION LINE, BACK TO SEE HOW, WHERE AND FROM WHAT IT IS MADE?

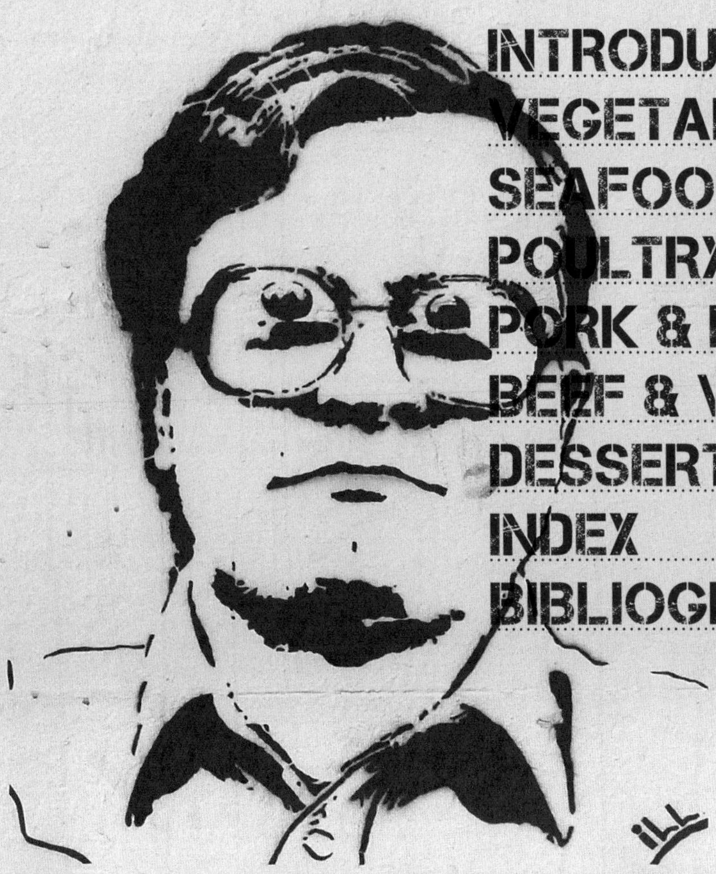

COOKING AND EATING FOR A SUSTAINABLE FUTURE

EACH DAY WE WAKE; THE NEW DAY WITH ALL ITS PROMISE IS YET TO UNFOLD. SLEEPY THOUGHTS. WE WASH OUR FACES AND LOOK INTO THE MIRROR AND COLLECTIVELY ORDER AND PLAN OUR DAY. BREAKFAST: FAST OR SLOW? KIDS? IS IT MY TURN TO DROP THEM OFF? WHAT ARE THEY HAVING FOR LUNCH? LIFE. LIFE IS BUSY. CAN WE SLOW DOWN WITHOUT JUMPING OFF THE TREADMILL? NO WAY! IS THAT THE TIME? I'M LATE FOR WORK ...

I am the father of two beautiful children. I am a chef in a busy restaurant that I run with my partner, Pauline, and her brother, Luke. Like all of you, I think, I plan and I juggle. I siphon and filter all the messages we receive in this media-fuelled age. What we should or shouldn't eat, do, dream or aspire to be. The pace of life kicks on; it is unrelenting. But is this really how we would like our lives to run?

When I first conceived the idea for this book, the breadth and scale of its theme seemed overwhelming. I wanted to write a book that provided straightforward answers to the questions many people have about how our food is produced; to consider the ethics of food production and whether or not the way we produce our food is sustainable. Then I'd contemplate the big issue of the day: the carbon footprint — the amount of carbon that is released into the atmosphere while growing, nurturing and producing the food that nourishes us. Nourishes us? Yes, the food that sustains our bodies and minds — real food not kilojoules, proteins, carbohydrates and fats.

Most urban chefs struggle to know the provenance of their produce. Chefs are in the business of satisfying customers, and to achieve this, good produce is generally the foundation of their success. Produce should be seasonal and at its prime, but you don't need to know how it's grown to keep most customers happy. Produce can simply be a list of ingredients that are replaced daily, depending on what was sold, by a simple telephone call to a providore. A chef could very well use the providore in much the same way you can wander the aisles of a supermarket and purchase what you need for dinner, without considering the origins or sustainability of what you have bought. I'm not suggesting for a moment that a chef or, indeed, the home cook doesn't consider this, but for too long the main consideration has been the price of our food.

When raw produce tastes good, a skilled chef applies the appropriate technique to accentuate and complement the flavours in a dish. Cooking is an historic and noble art, but cooking with an understanding of how the ingredients are grown and the impact that has on the environment will create a sustainable future. This topic is enormous and, at times, I admit I struggled through the quagmire of opinion while writing this book, as passions on this subject run raw. In the end, my goal was to encourage real food conversations that extend beyond the price and taste of the produce on the plate.

We have allowed our food production system to be run by huge corporations. Today it is all about economy of scale and ultimately the price of the end product. The cheap price of our food comes at a cost to the animals in our food system and the environment as a whole.

With a greater occurrence of obesity and type 2 diabetes both here in Australia and in other parts of the world, we really need to stop and take a look at what we eat and how we live our lives. Our modern Western diet has increasingly led us away from the wholesome foods our parents and grandparents ate. In their place, more and more processed convenience foods line the supermarket shelves and freezers. But I don't believe all is lost. Thankfully, more of us are starting to question what exactly is in the food we eat. What is hydrolysed fat and cochineal 120 or preservative 221? What is being added to our foods to make them last longer? Is it all about the money — cheap kilojoules and a fast buck — not wholesome, sustainably grown food? When I say 'sustainably' I mean it in the broadest context of the word. We must think sustainably for our bodies, our well-being and all living things in our environment.

In this book there are recipes to be made and food to be enjoyed; not too many ingredients in any one recipe mind you, because good food does not need to be complicated; in fact, I have carefully crafted the recipes to let the ingredients shine. This means, in most cases, you can easily and quickly prepare a nourishing, flavour-packed meal for the family without getting bogged down with complicated cooking techniques.

The vegetable chapter contains the greatest number of recipes and I've done this deliberately. Traditionally, when we conceive an idea for a meal we first decide on the meat protein component and then we choose the accompanying vegetables. I want to challenge this notion by encouraging you to choose the vegetables first. Draw inspiration from the seasonal produce displayed on your greengrocer's shelves, and only then decide on the protein. This is also why the photographs of the 'meat' in these chapters are exactly that: beautiful photographs of ethically produced animal protein on a plate. I didn't want any visual vegetable cues in the photographs that might tempt you to source ingredients that are out of season as you go about re-creating the dish.

And while you are preparing some of these recipes, or maybe in a quiet moment, take a bit of time to contemplate just how the fruit and vegetables, fish, poultry, pork, lamb and beef that form the ingredients in these recipes made their way to your supermarket or providore's shelves and, ultimately, your dinner table.

It is time for each one of us to take responsibility for our health, look at what we eat and what we truly value. As a father, chef and health fanatic, it is my hope that this book will affirm what you already believe: that good food, sustainably and ethically grown, is worth paying for.

MY OBSESSION WITH CYCLING AND FLY-FISHING TAKES ME AWAY FROM MY FAMILY REGULARLY. THESE PURSUITS ARE NECESSARY FOR MY MENTAL HEALTH, BUT THEIR TOLL ON MY FAMILY LIFE PALES IN COMPARISON TO THE COMMITMENT AND DEDICATION NEEDED TO PRODUCE A BODY OF TEXT AND RECIPES. WRITING IS TRULY THE MOST SELF-ABSORBING, SELFISH, STRESSFUL AND INDULGENT EXERCISE ANYONE CAN UNDERTAKE.

I thank my partner, Pauline, for her unfaltering love, wisdom and patience. This hasn't been an easy journey for us. During its course we have had dear friends pass away and relationships tested. Time lost cannot be replaced. But this book is about creating a better future. Hope and light always prevail, and we welcomed our son, Jethro, into this world. To my daughter, Mia, I thank you for providing me with the inspiration for this book and I promise to throw away the 'bloody' computer for the next 12 months at least!

I thank the team at Red Lantern for putting up with me during this process. I thank my mate Andrew de Sousa for his recipe inspiration and food preparation, Michelle Noerianto for her intelligent food styling, and Cath Muscat for her quest for perfection. Kim Rowney, my editor, I thank you for your guidance and craftsmanship. And of course the entire team at Murdoch Books — Reuben, you are the man.

VEGE

CONTENTS

TABLES 11

TO EAT THE FOOD PRODUCED BY
FARMERS WHO VALUE AND WORK
WITH NATURE IS TO ENJOY FOOD THAT
NOURISHES MORE THAN THE BODY — IT
IS FOOD PRODUCED TO REPLENISH THE
SOIL AND ENSURE FUTURE PRODUCTION
FOR THE GENERATIONS THAT FOLLOW.

Brisbane Valley
Organics

VEGETABLES

I BLAME MY GRANDFATHER FOR MY OBSESSION WITH SOIL. POP IS THE ONE WHO TAUGHT ME THAT SOIL IS COMPOSED OF ORGANIC AND INORGANIC MATERIALS — MICROORGANISMS, NUTRIENTS AND ROCKS — WHICH ARE BROKEN DOWN OVER TIME INTO PEBBLES, SAND AND CLAY. AS CHILDREN WE ATE IT, WE PLAYED IN IT AND WE MADE MUD PIES WITH IT.

Pop had a large and incredibly productive vegetable garden in his backyard. He never sold any of the produce; Grandma sliced, diced, boiled, baked and steamed the vegetables from his garden to feed their large family of eight. My parents also helped fuel my interest in growing vegetables for the family table — I have grown some of the best tomatoes, zucchini and eggplants I have ever eaten — and encouraged my fascination with the composition of soil and the intricacies of compost. Soil is, after all, the foundation on which all things grow.

Pop taught me that agriculture, by a simple definition, is the process of growing flavoursome and nutritious food. In order to achieve this goal various physical aspects have to be considered: among them the topography and annual rainfall of the area and, most importantly, the soil. The soil composition determines what sort of crops can be grown and where. To grow abundant fruit and vegetables year after year requires skill and knowledge. Typically the success of the crop depends on how well you can maintain the structure of the soil.

I encourage you to try and grow some of your own food for the table. I understand that not everyone has an expansive backyard, but you don't necessarily need one. With a good organic soil mixture, some compost and an understanding of the relationship between soil, sunlight and water, you'd be amazed at what you can grow in boxes on a balcony or in a courtyard. I'm not suggesting you will become self-sufficient, but what you will learn from the experience, if you take the time to contemplate, is an appreciation of the skilled farmers who grow vegetables on a commercial scale. And if you get the mix of the soil just right and maintain it throughout the seasons, the fruit and vegetables you grow will taste like no other — so fresh and full of flavour — and you can then choose whether to use pesticides on them or not.

SUPERMARKET PRODUCE

Most people buy their produce from big supermarket chains that, in turn, buy their fruit and vegetables from conventional farmers, who use synthetic fertilisers and petrochemical pesticides. Conventional farmers produce the majority of our food, but in the future I wonder if they will continue to do so, given their utter dependence on petroleum for their crop and soil management. The produce they grow is arguably as nutritious as vegetables grown by other means, but for me there are more sustainable ways to produce crops while simultaneously nurturing the soil and promoting environmental health.

Organic vegetables — vegetables grown without synthetic fertilisers and petrochemicals — are starting to appear on supermarket shelves, although the range is somewhat limited. I am suspicious of the supermarkets' intentions; I can't decide whether the organic presence is a tokenistic attempt to increase their 'green credentials' or a legitimate, fledgling effort to bring organic produce into the fold. That said, I'd still encourage you to buy organic if you are already in the habit of shopping there. The simple act of buying organic produce means you care. You care about the food you eat and how it is produced. If enough people buy organic produce then a greater range will be offered and, as a consequence, the vegetables will become more economical.

If you are truly interested in organic or locally grown fruit and vegetables, there are more rewarding ways to source and buy them. I find independent greengrocers and farmers' markets allow you to get up close and personal with the origins of your food, and the produce is usually a great deal fresher.

THE POWER OF THE SUPERMARKETS

Supermarkets are the major buyers of fruit and vegetables in Australia, having a 70 per cent share of the marketplace. They have the ability to set the price and buy produce in bulk, sometimes to the detriment of the smaller greengrocers. My local greengrocer, Joe, has complained to me on numerous occasions that he was unable to buy certain produce because the supermarkets had already bought it. 'They only left the inferior stuff, the produce I wouldn't dream of putting on my shelves,' he says. In theory, this is great news, as long as your supermarket shopping trip coincides with the delivery of fresh produce, but after the initial delivery, excess stock is then stored under refrigeration, to be dispatched to the supermarket as required over the following weeks.

Some farmers enter into contracts with supermarkets to supply vegetables of a certain size, colour and shape. Farming is a tough business; you can't blame the farmer for wanting to ensure his livelihood. Those of you who have ever grown a carrot at home will appreciate that uniform size and shape is not always in nature's plan. So what happens to all the misshapen vegetables? They are thrown away! There is absolutely nothing wrong with their flavour or nutritional value, but we are put off by the way they look. Put bluntly, if it doesn't look good, we won't buy it. You'd think, at the very least, these vegetables could find a home inside a tin but, to my knowledge, because of the nature of their contracts with supermarkets, farmers are unable to sell excess produce to anyone else. It seems society's admiration for the physically beautiful extends to fruit and vegetables too, and we overlook the more peculiarly formed produce simply because we don't appreciate its uniqueness.

FOOD MILES

Fruit and vegetables destined for the supermarket are harvested, sorted then packed for transportation. Typically the produce is taken by truck to a central warehouse. Here it's stored in huge refrigerators until it is distributed to the numerous supermarkets across the state. Finally, it will make its way to your dinner table. The length of time food is kept under refrigeration and the distance it travels within the distribution system, from the paddock to your plate, all contributes to its carbon footprint, often referred to as 'food miles'. In the United Kingdom, some supermarkets now print this information on food labels, showing the consumer the distance the produce has travelled.

The most sustainable way to shop is to buy locally grown seasonal produce, but this is not always possible. There is a food movement that suggests we should only eat what can be grown within a 100-mile (160-kilometre) radius of where we live. This sounds wonderful in theory but is not always practical, especially if you live in a large city. Not all of what we enjoy eating and drinking can be locally produced. I for one cannot make it through my day without a cup (or two) of coffee. Importing food from interstate and around the world is a fact of life. That said, we should still endeavour to choose our produce wisely. The further the produce has had to travel, the more fuel is used, and the more time it has spent in cold storage.

SEASONAL PRODUCE

When it comes to fruit and vegetables you have to question why supermarkets stock what they do. It would appear, at first glance, that there's enough variety of fresh produce to satisfy even the most discerning gourmand. However, if you look closely, you'll notice that not all of the produce is locally produced or, more importantly, in harmony with the season. In general our society is out of touch with the rhythm of nature, and it is easy to see why. Over the last decade or so, a proliferation of imported produce has surreptitiously invaded the fresh produce aisles of our supermarkets and greengrocers. Now we just expect these fruits and vegetables to be available throughout the majority of the year, even if the quality is somewhat sacrificed. With the prevailing attitude of instant gratification — I want to eat whatever I want, whenever I want — we have created our own produce paradox. We are too impatient to wait for the passing of the seasons.

The whole methodology of growing food has changed. Produce is now grown to be easily transported without damage and to look good on the shelf. This often means it is picked before it is fully ripened. Certain fruits will ripen once picked, but even though the fruit may become softer to the touch — we have probably all squeezed the life out of a plum or peach before buying one — it is debatable whether the flavour is anywhere near its full potential. A dear friend who owned a farm in Tasmania once said to me, 'If you want to know when produce is at its prime ask the farmer when he would harvest it for his table. He knows what a ripe piece of fruit or a vegetable looks like and when the time is right to eat it.' This philosophy is driving the farmers' market revolution in our capital cities.

PROVENANCE

Most of the food I eat is grown out of the soil, not chemically engineered in a laboratory. I follow the old adage of quality over quantity and pay special attention to whether the food I eat is ethically and sustainably produced. But how do we know if the produce we buy is produced in this manner? There is precious little information displayed at the point of sale in our supermarkets. Not much is listed beyond the obligatory 'produce of Australia' or 'imported product' sticker printed beside the price per kilogram sign. And there doesn't appear to be a food provenance chapter in the staff-training manual either! Have you ever asked a supermarket team member a question about the fresh produce and got an accurate answer?

For many people, the best way to shop is to buy directly from the grower or from a wholesaler. I try to maintain only one degree of separation from the food I eat — this is easier done than it may sound, as growers' markets are sprouting in the city faster than the first peas in spring. Fresh produce bought from a farmers' market is vital; it's full of flavour and essential nutrients. The produce is either harvested that morning or, at worse, the previous afternoon.

Throughout time, the marketplace has provided the setting for city dwellers to meet and talk to farmers. The market is not a place to be shy — step up, talk to the farmer and ask questions; you'll find they are more than happy to talk about their produce. Ask where the produce is grown. Ask if it was grown using sustainable farming methods. The more questions you ask, the richer the experience will be.

If you don't have access to a farmers' market, shop around for a good greengrocer like my friend Joe. He knows what is available and where his produce comes from. Like most neighbourhood storeowners he is always up for a chat. We are two passionate people who often banter about the price difference between locally grown conventional produce and organic produce. He doesn't understand why I choose to pay more for organic when I could buy his fresh conventional produce at a much cheaper price. I don't believe conversations about food production should always centre on price. If we removed food subsidies, added the environmental cost and the dividends paid to shareholders to the price of conventional produce, organic food would not only be price competitive, but we would be eating food grown with far less toxic chemicals.

POLYCULTURE

Organic farming, or polyculture, is a method of farming that emphasises and promotes the relationships that exist between all living things. Organic farming encourages biodiversity where all things live in harmony and move to the natural rhythm of life; it works with nature rather than trying to control it with chemicals. When it comes to horticulture it is proven we can grow vast amounts of fruit and vegetables without chemicals; humans have been doing this for centuries. The ancient Romans would cut down and burn woodlands and then plough the ash and charcoal back into the soil, enriching it with carbon before cultivating their food crops. They knew the importance of growing complementary crops for weed control and had learned the benefits of manure and its associated organisms. Cattle were allowed to graze on fallow land as crops were rotated from paddock to paddock. Although not always successful, the Romans formulated holistic farming methods in an attempt to ensure the long-term sustainability and productivity of the land.

Organic farming combines holistic and biological methods to maintain the health and productivity of the farm or ecosystem. To judge the success of a farm simply by observing what happens above ground is misleading, for this only shows half the picture. Artificial fertilisers and pesticides can't be seen. For sustainable and productive land management, a farmer must encourage beneficial insects, microbes and a healthy earthworm population. The humble earthworm is the unsung hero of our agriculture industry. Their subterranean contribution to the success of the harvest is crucial. The worms move through the soil, aerating it, thereby optimising the root absorption of nutrients and minerals.

On an organic farm, the soil is maintained and enriched by using beneficial groundcover plants and composted organic materials. Keeping the ground covered with vegetation helps store and draw carbon down into the soil and also prevents weeds from taking hold. Crucially, fields are rested in between crops so the soil can regain its potency, and crops are rotated. Because different crops take different elements and minerals from the soil, the soil is never depleted and maintains its vitality. Needless to say organic farmers have no need for artificial pesticides or fertilisers.

MONOCULTURE

Intensive horticulture is a relatively new farming phenomenon and is often referred to as monoculture. (This is how the majority of conventional vegetables are grown.) As the name suggests, it concentrates on growing the same variety of a single vegetable species on a defined area of land. It is highly mechanised, requiring minimal labour and is alarmingly dependent on fertilisers and pesticides. Examples of vegetables and plants grown in this manner are potatoes, corn, wheat, soy and the environmentally insidious palm tree. Palm oil is now used in everything from soap to food and bio-fuel, and is a major contributor to global deforestation.

Monoculture was created to streamline the agricultural process. It does this by concentrating its resources to achieve a single goal. It attempts to grow the greatest amount of produce per hectare of land in the most economical way, but has achieved this at great environmental expense. Science has played a large role in the development and 'success' of intensive horticulture.

THE HARMFUL EFFECTS OF SYNTHETIC FERTILISERS

On an intensive farm, less emphasis is placed on maintaining natural soil health and more is placed on the use of synthetic fertilisers, which are made up of nitrogen, phosphorus and potassium. These are all naturally occurring minerals vital for plant health, but unfortunately the manufacture of these artificial fertilisers is very energy intensive and is not sustainable. Phosphorus and potassium are mined, extracted from a finite resource, and atmospheric nitrogen needs to be converted into a plant-soluble form. This process requires the use of a significant amount of fossil fuel.

The environmental damage caused by these fertilisers and pesticides can be far-reaching, and once applied to the soil they are difficult to contain. The chemicals can wash off the crops and find their way into rivers or leach into the water table. Once in the rivers, the build-up of nitrogen from the fertiliser encourages destructive algal blooms. Farmers try to retain run-off water by building embankments around their crops, but unfortunately chemicals still find their way into the water system.

GENETICALLY MODIFIED (GM) PLANTS

Scientists have genetically modified the seeds of some vegetables to promote more favourable characteristics. Everything from disease resistance right through to water efficiency is enhanced to ensure maximum yields. These plants all become genetically identical. Some scientists are worried about this lack of gene diversity and are concerned GM vegetables won't be able to fight off or adapt to exposure from unexpected pathogens. Our long-term food security will be compromised if we lose the biodiversity that exists today. The increasing promotion of monoculture and GM fruit and vegetables is alarming, and this will be an ever-present concern into the future. Ultimately, all plants and animals depend on their genetic diversity for their long-term survival.

Genetic science and manufactured fertilisers and pesticides have enabled farmers to push the limit of what can be sustainably produced on a single plot of land. Increased crop yields have come at significant expense to the environment, the economy and, most importantly, our health. Food Standards Australia New Zealand (FSANZ) sets a minimum time between the spraying of pesticide and the harvesting of food crops. By the time we eat conventional produce the chemical residue is meant to be negligible. This may be so, but I prefer to eat vegetables grown without chemicals or, at the very least, vegetables with minimal pesticide exposure. Even produce grown by the most conscientious organic farmer could in all likelihood contain traces of pesticide.

Today, some people believe good farming practice is achieved when as much produce as possible is harvested from a defined area of land, regardless of the chemical inputs. Monsanto is a multinational company that produces GM seeds and agricultural chemicals for commercial-scale food production. Some farmers have signed contracts to use their products exclusively. But only now do many realise what they have done. Unfortunately, these farmers have bought a ticket to board the chemical train that is fast running out of control. They are unable, even if willing, to disembark and revert back to a more sustainable way of farming.

There is now the real danger of GM food crops making their way into our food system. Monsanto and its subsidiaries are responsible for engineering GM food crops. This could be seen as a stroke of genius or the work of the devil, depending on where you sit in this debate. It can be seen as a natural extension of what man has been doing since he first domesticated wild plants for food production or, as many believe, it is a line that should have never been crossed. These plants are scientifically designed for specific traits such as drought, pest and pathogen resilience and, in the case of the tomato, the ability to be fully ripened without being soft and squishy. The growing of GM food crops will continue to be very controversial.

In the United States, some farmers who use GM crops have had to resort to physically ripping horse weed (an example of a herbicide-resistant 'super weed') out of the ground by hand. Farmers who grow GM crops use herbicides that are designed to kill the weeds but leave the crop healthy. In this case, the GM food crop has remained resistant to the herbicide, but unfortunately the weeds have adapted to resist it as well. If the farmer uses another brand of herbicide to kill the weeds he runs the risk of killing the food crop. This situation is frightening and the only way to stop the cycle of stronger and stronger chemical use is to do exactly that: STOP IT. This is a classic example of man trying to circumvent nature and only succeeding in making matters worse.

CREATING A BETTER FUTURE

Australia might well be the lucky country but it is also a very dry one; climate change will only exacerbate this situation. Over a decade of drought has forced the agricultural industry to change the way it uses water. Irrigators have bought themselves a little time by switching to a drip irrigation system, which reduces water loss through evaporation.

Our agricultural landscape is changing. As temperatures rise, the climate of the tropical north will extend further south. Rainfall will become less predictable and the rise in temperature and the resulting clear skies will produce more crop-destroying frosts. Climate change will see a seismic shift in where and how our food is produced.

But it's not all bad news; some farmers will actually benefit from global warming. The irony is that some species of plants, such as lettuce, tomatoes and beans, will benefit from an extended growing season with rising temperatures, but others, that rely on the cool night for crop growth, will obviously be disadvantaged. Perennial crops like apples and pears and the deciduous fruit and nut tree industries will be hit hard. These trees rely on the cooler weather to break their winter dormancy. Farmers will have to adapt to these new conditions; some may have to move to more favourable areas. The quality, size, price and, dare I say, flavour will be affected by the unpredictability of the weather and we will have to accept this. In my lifetime, there is every possibility that I will say to my grandchildren, 'This is not how an apple tasted back when I was young.'

I believe biodynamic and organic farmers will finally receive the recognition they deserve and be the horticulture champions of the future. These farmers promote biodiversity and encourage many different and distinct organisms to work together for a common cause. Imagine if our society could do the same — to promote a society that lives in harmony with nature; one that works with nature rather than trying to control it. It is a plan I would be happy to be a part of.

Climate change will present many challenges and we will need to find sustainable creative solutions. Perhaps the journey to promote a better future starts with changing the way we shop. Buy locally grown produce from farmers who care for the environment. Fruit and vegetables do not have to be perfectly formed to be nutritious, however they do need to be grown with consideration for the environment and the generations that follow. Not only will we be promoting biodiversity, but by buying organic or biodynamic produce, we reduce the production and use of chemicals and encourage sustainable farming practices.

EAT YOUR GREENS!

SOUND FAMILIAR? MANY OF US ARE BORN WITH AN INHERENT DISLIKE OF GREENS, BUT WITH MUM'S PERSUASION (SHE ALWAYS KNOWS BEST!) WE EVENTUALLY ACCEPT THEY EXIST FOR OUR BENEFIT. I'M ATTEMPTING TO 'REBRAND' THE VEGETABLE AND MAKE IT THE HERO OF THIS BOOK. VEGETABLES GROWN WITH CARE, FREE FROM CHEMICALS AND PICKED IN THEIR PRIME RADIATE GOODNESS. UNFORTUNATELY, THEY ARE GENERALLY THE AFTERTHOUGHT, ONLY GIVEN CONSIDERATION ONCE THE MEAT COMPONENT OF THE MEAL HAS BEEN DECIDED.

The vegetable recipes within this chapter have been loosely grouped seasonally, into spring and summer vegetables in the first half, and autumn and winter vegetables in the second half. Some are complete delicious meals, but the majority are side dishes to be matched to the meat and seafood recipes that follow.

I'd like you to consider eating your greens and possibly having one, if not two, vegetarian meals a week. Sustainably caught seafood, organic and free-range poultry, pork, lamb and beef are commonly perceived as expensive, although by the time you have finished reading this book I hope I have succeeded in convincing you that 'expensive' is not always quantified in dollar value. Somewhere along the line, someone or something pays the real cost of production. Unfortunately, it is usually the animals on intensive farms or the environment that pays that price. Value for money is another thing altogether.

Eating a couple of vegetarian meals a week offers true value for money and you reduce your environmental footprint in the process. The money saved (I'm now speaking to all carnivores) from eating vegetables could then be spent on truly flavoursome, ethically and sustainably produced meat products. When you buy free-range or organic meat, you are encouraging and supporting farmers who truly nurture and value the domestic animals in their care.

Ethically produced fruit and vegetables are to be enjoyed and celebrated. Meals enjoyed with friends are to be treasured. Mix and match the recipes in this chapter with the seafood and meat recipes to suit the season and the occasion.

MARINATED SUMMER RADISHES WITH CURRANTS, MINT & CHIVE DRESSING

6 SERVES / SIDE DISH

1 bunch of radishes (6–8 radishes)
1 celery stalk
200 g (7 oz) baby (pattypan) yellow squash
100 g (3½ oz) dried currants
juice of 1 lemon
1 teaspoon dijon mustard

125 ml (4 fl oz/½ cup) good-quality virgin
    olive oil
½ bunch of chives
12 mint leaves
1 long red chilli, seeded and cut into
    julienne

Top and tail the radishes, then cut them into thin wedges by continually halving the radish until you get wedges about 5 mm (¼ inch) thick. Cut the celery on the diagonal into 2 mm (¹⁄₁₆ inch) wide slices. Slice the yellow squash into 2 mm (¹⁄₁₆ inch) thick pieces.

   Place the currants in a bowl, cover with hot water and soak for 10 minutes, then drain. Place the currants and all the vegetables in a bowl and set aside. In a separate bowl, combine the lemon juice with the mustard, then mix in the olive oil and season with sea salt and freshly ground black pepper. Finely slice the chives (reserving a few for garnish) and mint, then fold them through the dressing. Lightly toss the dressing through the vegetables and allow them to marinate for 30 minutes before serving. Garnish with the reserved chives and the chilli.

24

ALTHOUGH RADISHES ARE AVAILABLE YEAR-ROUND, THEIR PEAK SEASON IS FROM SPRING TO AUTUMN. SUMMER RADISHES ARE CRISP AND JUICY, PERFECT FOR EATING RAW IN SALADS.

SAUTÉ OF FRESH SPRING PEAS IN LEMON BUTTER

6 SERVES / SIDE DISH

250 g (9 oz) snow peas (mangetout)
250 g (9 oz) sugar snap peas
200 g (7 oz) shelled peas (you will need about 800 g/1 lb 12 oz unshelled peas)
100 g (3½ oz) good-quality butter
1 teaspoon crushed garlic
2½ tablespoons lemon juice

150 g (5½ oz) dried ricotta cheese (see Note)
finely grated zest of ½ lemon
1 tablespoon chopped parsley
2 teaspoons chopped oregano
1 long red chilli, seeded and chopped

Top and tail the snow peas and sugar snaps and set them aside with the shelled peas. Put just enough water to cook the vegetables in a saucepan, add a generous pinch of salt and bring the water to the boil. Have a bowl of iced water ready to refresh the vegetables. Add the snow peas, sugar snaps and peas to the boiling water and cook for 2 minutes, then drain and refresh in the iced water. Once cooled, pour the vegetables into a colander and shake dry.

Place a frying pan over high heat and add the butter. When the butter melts, add the garlic, then as soon as the butter starts to bubble, add the vegetables, tossing them in the pan to heat through and coat in the butter. Add the lemon juice, toss well, then season with sea salt and freshly ground black pepper. Transfer to a serving platter, crumble the ricotta over the vegetables and garnish with the lemon zest, herbs and chilli.

Note: Dried ricotta is a firmer version of fresh ricotta, with a mild sweet flavour and an added hint of salt. You can find it in Italian delicatessens or specialist cheese stores.

WHEN COOKING OR BLANCHING VEGETABLES, THINK AHEAD AND CONSIDER HOW YOU CAN CAPTURE AND REUSE THE COOKING WATER. PERHAPS IT COULD BE USED TO COOK SOMETHING ELSE OR COOLED AND USED TO WATER YOUR HERB GARDEN.

FOR THIS RECIPE I HAVE STEAMED THE EGGS IN A MICROWAVE. THIS MAY SEEM A LITTLE UNUSUAL, BUT MICROWAVE OVENS PRODUCE ONE-THIRD LESS GREENHOUSE GASES THAN A CONVENTIONAL ELECTRIC STOVETOP.

CHARGRILLED ASPARAGUS WITH STEAMED BIODYNAMIC EGGS

4 SERVES / STARTER OR BREAKFAST

3 bunches of asparagus (about 24 spears)
good-quality Australian olive oil
4 organic and biodynamic eggs, 65–70 g
   (2¼–2½ oz) each

½ quantity of poor man's parmesan
   (page 36)

Wash and dry the asparagus, then lay them out on a chopping board. Line the tips of the asparagus up with the side of the board, then cut off the woody stems (the bottom 2–4 cm/¾–1½ inches) on the diagonal. Brush about 1 tablespoon of olive oil over the asparagus, coating them evenly and liberally, then set aside.

To steam the eggs, first grease the inside of four individual microwave-safe containers with a little olive oil (microwave-safe coffee cups are ideal). Break the eggs into the containers and then pierce the yolk with the tip of a sharp knife; this prevents the eggs from exploding. Cover the containers with damp paper towel, then place all four eggs on the microwave plate. Set the microwave to low power and cook the eggs for 5 minutes (I use 30 per cent power and give them 2 minutes, then 1 minute at a time, checking them after every minute, for a total of 5 minutes).

Preheat a chargrill pan over medium heat. While the eggs are cooking, place the asparagus in the hot pan and cook for 2 minutes, then roll them over and cook for a further 2 minutes.

Divide the asparagus among the serving plates. Gently centre an egg on the asparagus and scatter a generous amount of poor man's parmesan over the top. Lightly season with sea salt, freshly ground black pepper and a little olive oil.

GNOCCHI WITH ROASTED CHERRY TOMATO SAUCE

6 SERVES / MAIN

GNOCCHI

1 kg (2 lb 4 oz) medium-sized bintje
    potatoes (or use desiree or nicola),
    unpeeled
100 g (3½ oz/⅔ cup) plain (all-purpose)
    flour, plus 35 g (1¼ oz/¼ cup) extra
1 egg
40 g (1½ oz) butter
¾ teaspoon salt
freshly ground white pepper

ROASTED CHERRY TOMATO SAUCE

500 g (1 lb 2 oz) cherry tomatoes, scored
    across the top
1 small leek, white part only, washed well
    and cut into fine rings
4 garlic cloves, finely chopped
1 or 2 bird's eye chillies, finely sliced
100 ml (3½ fl oz) olive oil
2½ tablespoons red wine vinegar
½ bunch of thyme

Preheat the oven to 180°C (350°F/Gas 4). To make the gnocchi, bake the whole potatoes for 30–40 minutes, or until they are soft. Test for doneness by inserting a knife into the potato. If the knife passes through the potato with ease, it is done. Remove the potatoes from the oven and allow to cool slightly. Peel the potatoes, then pass through a mouli into a large bowl, or crush with a potato masher. Do not overwork the potato or the gnocchi will become too chewy. When the potato is cool, add the flour, egg, butter, salt and white pepper and gently work the mixture as you would if you were making bread dough. Knead the potato for a couple of minutes, then cover with a damp cloth and allow it to rest for 30 minutes (it will be a very soft dough).

Reduce the oven to 160°C (315°F/Gas 2–3). To make the roasted cherry tomato sauce, place the tomatoes, leek, garlic, chilli, olive oil, vinegar and thyme (leaves and stalks) in an ovenproof frying pan or dish. Season with a little sea salt and freshly ground black pepper, then cover loosely with non-stick baking paper and foil. Roast in the oven for 30 minutes, then remove the cover and continue to roast for 15 minutes to reduce the sauce slightly and to give the tomatoes a little colour. Remove the pan from the oven. The tomatoes should have collapsed; if not, gently push down on them with a potato masher. Check the seasoning and stir to combine.

Scatter the extra flour over the work surface, then divide the potato dough into four. Roll each portion into long sausage shapes, about 2 cm (¾ inch) wide. With a sharp knife, cut the dough into 3 cm (1¼ inch) long pieces. Bring a large saucepan of salted water to the boil, add half the gnocchi and cook until they float to the surface. Remove with a slotted spoon, drain off any excess water and place into serving bowls. Repeat with the remaining gnocchi. Spoon the roasted cherry tomato sauce over the gnocchi and serve.

This gnocchi also goes well with the sautéed mushrooms with French shallots (page 55), or whatever sauce you fancy.

THIS DISH WAS INSPIRED BY THE PROVENCAL CLASSIC, PAN BAGNAT. IT'S TRADITIONALLY MADE FROM A HOLLOWED-OUT LOAF OF BREAD FILLED WITH SALADE NICOISE, BUT YOU OFTEN SEE OTHER VERSIONS MADE WITH ROASTED AND CHARGRILLED VEGETABLES. I'VE TAKEN THE IDEA OF USING THE BREAD AND CHARGRILLED VEGETABLES, BUT LAYERED THEM INTO A DISH INSTEAD.

EGGPLANT & MOZZARELLA BAKE

6 SERVES / MAIN

185 ml (6 fl oz/¾ cup) olive oil
2 eggplants (aubergines), cut into
   1 cm (½ inch) thick slices
1 loaf of stale sourdough or ciabatta bread
1 quantity tomato sauce (recipe below)

1 large handful of basil leaves, torn
300 g (10½ oz) buffalo mozzarella, torn
extra virgin olive oil, for drizzling
50 g (1¾ oz/½ cup) freshly grated
   parmesan cheese

Preheat the oven to 180°C (350°F/Gas 4). Heat 3 tablespoons of the olive oil in a large non-stick frying pan over medium heat. Add the eggplant in small batches and fry for 3 minutes on each side until lightly browned. Remove and drain on paper towel. Repeat this process with the oil and eggplant until all the eggplant is cooked.

Cut the bread into 5 mm (¼ inch) thick slices. Thoroughly oil a large, deep casserole dish. Cover the base of the dish with a single layer of bread, then cover the bread with a generous amount of tomato sauce and some basil. Place a layer of fried eggplant and mozzarella over the sauce, and drizzle with extra virgin olive oil. Continue to alternate the layers until all the ingredients have been used. Scatter over the parmesan, season with sea salt and freshly ground black pepper and bake for 30 minutes, or until golden. Serve with a green salad.

TOMATO SAUCE

2 tablespoons olive oil
1 onion, finely chopped
2 garlic cloves, crushed

800 ml (28 fl oz) tomato passata (puréed
   tomatoes) or use the equivalent of
   fresh, ripe or tinned tomatoes, puréed

Heat the olive oil in a frying pan over medium heat and fry the onion for 5 minutes until soft and translucent, then add the garlic and cook for 2 minutes. Stir through the tomato passata, bring to the boil, then reduce the heat and simmer for 10 minutes. Set aside until needed.

GREEN BEANS WITH SWEET RED CAPSICUMS & TOMATO SAUCE

6 SERVES / SIDE DISH

300 g (10½ oz) ripe tomatoes, peeled
   (see Note, page 104)
600 g (1 lb 5 oz) green beans
1 small red capsicum (pepper)

1 small onion
100 ml (3½ fl oz) olive oil
1 tablespoon crushed garlic
¼ teaspoon sweet smoked paprika

Dice the peeled tomatoes to yield 250 g (9 oz/1 cup). Top and tail the green beans, slice them in half on the diagonal, then place in a bowl. Cut the capsicum and onion into 5 mm (¼ inch) dice and set aside.

   Place a frying pan over medium heat and add half the olive oil. Add the onion, capsicum and garlic and gently fry until the onion and garlic just start to colour. Stir in the beans and continue to fry for 2 minutes. Stir through the tomato and remaining oil, cover the pan and simmer for 2–3 minutes. Before serving, season with the paprika and sea salt and freshly ground black pepper.

LEEKS BRAISED IN WHITE WINE & THYME

4 SERVES / SIDE DISH

2 bunches of small leeks (12 leeks)
250 ml (9 fl oz/1 cup) white wine
40 g (1½ oz) butter
¼ bunch of thyme

1 bay leaf
a pinch of sea salt
a pinch of white pepper

Preheat the oven to 160°C (315°F/Gas 2–3). Remove the roots and the outer layer of the leek, and trim off all the green leaves. Wash well. Cut the leeks into 4 cm (1½ inch) long pieces, then place them in a casserole dish with the wine, butter, thyme and bay leaf. Add the sea salt and white pepper and cover with a lid or foil. Place in the oven and cook for 20 minutes, or until the leeks are tender. Alternatively, this dish can be cooked for the same period of time in a flameproof casserole dish over low heat on the stovetop.

ZUCCHINI, TOMATO, OLIVE & FETA GRATIN

6 SERVES / SIDE DISH

500 g (1 lb 2 oz) very ripe roma (plum)
    tomatoes
1 kg (2 lb 4 oz) zucchini (courgettes)
4 tablespoons olive oil
1 large onion, chopped
6 garlic cloves, finely chopped

100 g (3 ½ oz) kalamata olives
200 g (7 oz) feta cheese, crumbled
1 handful of basil leaves
50 g (1¾ oz/½ cup) poor man's parmesan
    (recipe below)

Preheat the oven to 180°C (350°F/Gas 4). To peel the tomatoes, score a cross in the base of each tomato. Put the tomatoes in a heatproof bowl and cover with boiling water. Leave for 30–60 seconds, then refresh in a bowl of iced water. Peel the skin away from the cross and discard it. Quarter the tomatoes lengthways, then cut into 1 cm (½ inch) dice and set aside. Cut the zucchini into quarters lengthways, then cut into 1 cm (½ inch) dice.

Heat the olive oil in a large deep frying pan over medium heat and fry the onion and garlic for 10 minutes until slightly caramelised. Add the tomato, zucchini, olives, feta and basil, season with sea salt and freshly ground black pepper, and toss to combine the flavours. Transfer to a 3 litre (105 fl oz/12 cup) capacity ovenproof dish and cook for 30 minutes, or until the zucchini is tender. To serve, sprinkle with the poor man's parmesan.

POOR MAN'S PARMESAN MAKES 150 G (5 ½ OZ/1 ½ CUPS)

1 big handful of stale ciabatta bread
    without the crust
4 tablespoons olive oil
1 small new season onion, finely diced

1 garlic clove, finely chopped
finely grated zest of 1 lemon
½ bunch of parsley, finely chopped

Tear the bread into small pieces, about 1 cm (½ inch) cubed. Place a frying pan over medium heat and add the olive oil and onion. Gently fry the onion until soft and golden, then add the bread pieces and a little extra olive oil if necessary, and fry until the bread is crisp. Add the garlic and fry for 1 minute, then add the lemon zest, stir to combine, and fry for a further 2 minutes. Fold through the parsley and season with salt and freshly ground black pepper.

I DON'T KNOW THE EXACT ORIGINS OF 'POOR MAN'S PARMESAN' BUT THE STORY GOES LIKE THIS: TRADITIONALLY IN ITALY, PARMESAN CHEESE WAS VERY EXPENSIVE, SO THE PEASANTS CAME UP WITH THE IDEA OF USING FRIED BREADCRUMBS TO SPRINKLE OVER THEIR PASTA AND VEGETABLE DISHES. THIS MIXTURE OF GARLIC, ONION, HERBS AND BREAD IS SO FULL OF FLAVOUR AND CRUNCH THAT THE END RESULT SEEMS ALMOST DECADENT — NOT A DISH FOR A POOR MAN AT ALL!

♡ Coffee sm 3- lg 3·50
♡ Tea 3- ♡ Chai 3·50
♡ LSD latte soy dandelion 4-
♡ Hot chocolate sm 3 lg 3·5
♡ Belgian Hot choc sm 4·50
   white × milk × dark lg 5·50
♡ Milkshakes 4·50 vanilla
   caramel × strawberry × lime
   chocolate
   ♡ Smoothies 5·90 mango
   banana × raspberry × blueberry
♡ Icy fruit frappe 5·90
♡ San Pellegrino Mineral
   water - sm 3 - lg 6
♡ Iced coffee or choc 4·50
   ♡ Soy 50¢ extra ♡

w salmon 13·50 Hea
or bacon
   Breakf
♡ Fresh seasonal fr
♡ Organic muesli ñ r
      toasted or
♡ Turkish fruit toa
♡ toast - white, multig
♡ Buttermilk pancakes
♡ Mexican breakfast-
   roast capsicum, cor

♡ Omelette 1. Cho
          2. Mediterranea
♡ Free range eggs
♡ Extras 3- mushies
          hash brown
          4- smoked

SAUTÉED BROCCOLI, ANCHOVY & CHILLI TAGLIARINI

6 SERVES / MAIN

600 g (1 lb 5 oz) ready-made fresh
   egg tagliarini
500 g (1 lb 2 oz) broccoli
200 ml (7 fl oz) olive oil
1 small onion, finely diced
1 tablespoon crushed garlic

2 bird's eye chillies, finely sliced
6 anchovy fillets
finely grated zest and juice of 1 lemon
1 quantity of poor man's parmesan
   (page 36) or 100 g (3½ oz) of the real
   Parmigiano Reggiano

Pour 3 litres (105 fl oz/12 cups) of water into a large pot and add a small handful of salt. Cover the pot and bring to a rapid boil over high heat, then remove the lid, add the pasta and cook for 1–2 minutes. When the pasta is cooked, pour it into a colander set over a large bowl to reserve the water. Quickly rinse the pasta under cold running water until it is cool. Leave the pasta in the colander to drain and set aside.

Slice 5 mm (¼ inch) off the bottom of the broccoli stalk, then cut the stalk off just below the florets. You now have two sections: stalk and florets. Square off the edges of the stalk so you have four flat sides, to make it easier and safer to slice. Cut the stalk lengthways into 3 mm (⅛ inch) wide strips, then cut again lengthways to produce batons. Now slice it across to form 3 mm (⅛ inch) dice. Separate the florets and cut them as thinly as possible so they almost crumble apart.

Place the reserved pasta water back into a large pot, cover and bring to a rapid boil. Meanwhile, place a large frying pan over medium heat and add the olive oil. When the oil is hot, add the onion, garlic and diced broccoli stalk and cook until the broccoli is soft and the onion is golden. Blanch the broccoli florets in the boiling water for 2 minutes, drain, then quickly add to the frying pan, stirring well, and cook for a further 5 minutes.

Add the chilli, anchovies and lemon zest and juice to the pan and stir well to combine all the flavours. Increase the heat and add the pasta to the pan, stirring and tossing to coat the pasta with the sauce and to heat it through. Taste the sauce and season with sea salt and freshly ground black pepper. Portion the pasta into bowls and garnish with poor man's parmesan or the real stuff.

BROCCOLI IS GROWN WITH LITTLE CHEMICAL INTERVENTION, SO FAVOURING ORGANIC OVER CONVENTIONALLY GROWN PRODUCE WOULDN'T NECESSARILY BE WARRANTED EXCEPT ON AN ETHICAL BASIS. I SUGGEST YOU BUILD A RELATIONSHIP WITH YOUR SUPPLIER AND FIND OUT WHAT DAYS THEY GO TO THE MARKET AND THEN BUY YOUR FRUIT AND VEGETABLES ON THOSE DAYS.

CONVENTIONALLY GROWN LEAFY
GREENS SHOULD BE WASHED
THOROUGHLY. INSECTS FIND THEM
IRRESISTIBLE AND SO FARMERS
UNLEASH AN ARSENAL OF CHEMICAL
DETERRENTS TO CONTROL THEM.

GREEN TOMATO SALAD WITH LIME, PALM SUGAR & BLACK PEPPER DRESSING

6 SERVES / SIDE DISH

750 g (1 lb 10 oz) green tomatoes
1 Lebanese (short) cucumber, sliced in half
    lengthways and seeded
50 g (1¾ oz) red Asian shallots, finely sliced
2 long red chillies, seeded and finely sliced
2 kaffir lime (makrut) leaves, finely sliced

DRESSING
100 ml (3½ fl oz) lime juice
2 tablespoons fish sauce
75 g (2½ oz) palm sugar (jaggery), grated
2 teaspoons freshly ground black pepper

To make the dressing, put the lime juice and fish sauce into a bowl. Add the palm sugar and stir well to dissolve it. Add the pepper, stir well to combine the flavours, and set aside.

    Cut the core from the tomatoes, then cut the tomatoes into eight equal-sized wedges. Finely slice the cucumber halves. Combine the tomatoes, cucumber, Asian shallots, chilli and lime leaves in a large bowl. Stir through the dressing and allow the salad to marinate for 30 minutes before serving.

SUMMER LEAF & HERB SALAD

6 SERVES / SIDE DISH

200 g (7 oz) mizuna
100 g (3½ oz) picked watercress
1 handful of basil leaves
1 handful of mint leaves

1 small handful of Vietnamese mint leaves
2 spring onions (scallions), finely sliced
about 100 ml (3½ fl oz) Vietnamese salad
    dressing (page 44)

Wash the salad leaves and herbs well in cold water, then place them in a colander to dry, or use a salad spinner. Once dry, mix the salad leaves, herbs and spring onion in a bowl with the dressing, and serve.

CHARGRILLED JAPANESE EGGPLANT WITH DAIKON

6 SERVES / SIDE DISH

½ daikon
2 teaspoons salt
1 tablespoon sugar
100 ml (3½ fl oz) peanut oil, plus extra, for brushing
1 small onion, finely sliced
6 small Japanese eggplants (aubergines)

60 g (2¼ oz) crushed roasted peanuts
2 spring onions (scallions), finely sliced on the diagonal
1 large handful of coriander (cilantro) leaves
2 bird's eye chillies, finely sliced
Vietnamese salad dressing (recipe below)

Peel and grate the daikon on the coarse side of a vegetable grater. This should yield about 140 g (5 oz/1 cup) of grated daikon. Put it in a bowl with the salt and sugar and mix well. Set aside for 30 minutes, then squeeze and discard the juice from the daikon, reserving the flesh.

Pour the peanut oil into a heavy-based saucepan and heat to 180°C (350°F), or until a cube of bread dropped into the oil turns golden brown in 15 seconds. Fry the onion in two batches, stirring occasionally to prevent it from sticking together, until it is crisp and golden brown. Remove the onion from the oil and drain on paper towel.

Heat a chargrill pan over medium heat until hot. Halve the eggplants lengthways and brush liberally with the extra peanut oil. Chargrill for about 3 minutes each side, or until the flesh is soft (be careful not to burn the skin). Arrange the eggplant halves on a platter and top with the daikon, fried onion, peanuts, spring onion, coriander and chillies. Dress with the Vietnamese salad dressing. Serve hot or cold.

VIETNAMESE SALAD DRESSING MAKES 240 ML (8 FL OZ)

6 cm (2½ inch) piece of lemongrass, white part only, finely sliced
125 ml (4 fl oz/½ cup) pineapple juice
2 tablespoons light soy sauce

1 tablespoon rice vinegar
1 tablespoon caster (superfine) sugar
1 tablespoon chilli oil
2 teaspoons minced pickled red chilli

To make the dressing, put the lemongrass in a mortar and pestle and pound to form a smooth paste. Place into a small saucepan along with the pineapple juice, soy sauce, vinegar and sugar. Bring to the boil, then remove the pan from the heat. Stir through the chilli oil and pickled chilli and allow it to cool. The salad dressing can be kept for up to 4 days in the fridge.

USING LOCAL PRODUCE REDUCES THE
FOOD MILES, OR GREENHOUSE GAS
EMISSIONS, INCURRED IN TRANSPORTING IT
FROM THE FARM GATE TO YOU AT HOME.
YOU CAN ALSO TRY GROWING HERBS AND
VEGETABLES IN RECYCLED STYROFOAM
BOXES — IT IS EASY, FUN AND INVOLVES
SURPRISINGLY LITTLE MAINTENANCE.

SWEET & SOUR CAPSICUM, PINEAPPLE & BASIL

6 SERVES / SIDE DISH

1 large green capsicum (pepper)
1 large red capsicum (pepper)
1 onion
200 g (7 oz) peeled pineapple
2 large tomatoes
1 celery stalk

2 tablespoons vegetable oil
1 garlic clove, crushed
100 g (3½ oz) honey
2 tablespoons sugar
100 ml (3½ fl oz) rice vinegar
1 large handful of basil leaves

Dice the capsicums, onion, pineapple and tomatoes into 1 cm (½ inch) square pieces. Finely slice the celery on the diagonal.

Heat a wok or large frying pan over medium heat and add the oil. When the oil is hot but not smoking, add the onion and fry for 2 minutes. Add the garlic and capsicum and fry until the vegetables just start to soften and colour slightly. Add the pineapple, tomato and celery, then add the honey, sugar and vinegar. Cook for 5 minutes, stirring occasionally. Stir in the basil, then season with sea salt and freshly ground black pepper.

CUCUMBER & CELERY SALAD WITH YOGHURT DRESSING

6 SERVES / SIDE DISH

3 Lebanese (short) cucumbers, about 400 g
   (14 oz) in total
2 celery stalks
1 big handful of cherry tomatoes
1 long red chilli, seeded and finely sliced
2 tablespoons lemon juice

1 handful of coriander (cilantro) leaves,
   roughly chopped
1 teaspoon ground cumin
2 teaspoons sugar
¼ teaspoon sweet paprika
250 g (9 oz/1 cup) natural Greek yoghurt

Cut the cucumber into quarters lengthways, then align the lengths on your chopping board. Slice across the lengths at 1 cm (½ inch) intervals and set aside. Finely slice the celery and halve the cherry tomatoes. Place all of the ingredients, except the yoghurt, into a bowl and mix well. Add the yoghurt just prior to serving the salad, season with sea salt and freshly ground black pepper. Serve with pork, chicken or grilled fish.

WHAT I DO TO MAKE THE WORLD A BETTER PLACE

CLIMATE CHANGE AND ITS IMPACT ON THE PLANET IS OMNIPRESENT; IT IS THE MOST IMPORTANT ISSUE OF OUR TIME. I BELIEVE THE INDIVIDUAL CHOICES WE MAKE DAILY EITHER CONTRIBUTE TO, OR HELP REDUCE, THE WARMING OF OUR PLANET. THE MALAISE OF THE CLIMATE SCEPTICS SHOULD NOT INHIBIT OUR DESIRE TO ACT, FOR EVEN THE SMALLEST POSITIVE ACTION HAS THE POWER TO MANIFEST ITSELF INTO SUBSTANTIAL CHANGE. WHEN I FIRST BECAME A FATHER THIS BELIEF TRULY HIT HOME; I AM NOW COMMITTED TO MAKING INFORMED CHOICES, CHOICES THAT WILL BENEFIT MY FAMILY, THEIR FUTURE AND THE ENVIRONMENT.

We don't all have to become raging eco warriors, but what we can do is learn how our food is produced and, almost as importantly, shop wisely. I feel we should adopt a more Mediterranean approach to buying fruit and vegetables by buying less, more frequently, to reduce the chance of food being wasted. Every year we waste millions of tonnes of uneaten fresh produce. This not only represents an enormous waste of the farmers' time and energy, it literally means you are throwing money and valuable resources away. Stop for a moment and think about the environmental cost of our wastefulness, and consider all of the water and energy used in the production of the food we eat (or don't eat).

Produce that can no longer be eaten should be thoughtfully disposed of. Organic waste that is thrown into a regular garbage bin will end up in landfill. Here it will rot, over time breaking down into a toxic sludge, releasing harmful methane gas into the atmosphere. If that same rotting produce was placed in a compost bin and allowed to breathe, the presence of oxygen, worms and microbes will turn the waste produce into valuable organic fertiliser. I have a 400-kilogram compost bin out the back of the restaurant. We compost all of the vegetable scraps from the kitchen and I then use this dynamic organic fertiliser on our very modest garden. It is not difficult to set up a composting system at home. Local councils now provide compost bins and can also help you set up a worm farm, which is another environmental way of dealing with household food scraps. Again, it is the little things that we do that make all the difference.

I visit the organic fruit and vegetable market twice a week to buy fresh produce for Red Lantern. I also buy conventionally grown produce, which is delivered twice a week; typically this is the more boutique Asian herbs and vegetables that are grown by Vietnamese farmers just outside Sydney. All up, the restaurant receives fresh fruit and vegetables four times a week. This reduces the amount of refrigeration needed and guarantees the freshness of the produce. Another benefit is that waste is practically zero. In the restaurant business you don't make money out of the food you throw in the bin, and I've extended this philosophy to the amount of food I put on the plate.

To my knowledge, no one leaves Red Lantern hungry, but I'm always conscious of reducing the potential for waste. I continually try to balance the quantity of food served on the plate with meeting the customers' expectations. I believe it's not only what we eat but also the amount of food we eat that makes the difference to our health and to the environment.

GREEN PAPAYA SALAD WITH SNAKE BEANS & TOMATO

6 SERVES / SIDE DISH

1 small green papaya, peeled and shredded
  (see Note) (you'll need about 300 g/
  10½ oz shredded)
150 g (5½ oz) snake (yard-long) beans
250 g (9 oz) cherry tomatoes

2 large handfuls of mixed Asian herbs
125 ml (4 fl oz/½ cup) lime and chilli
  dressing (recipe below)
40 g (1½ oz/½ cup) fried Asian shallots
40 g (1½ oz/¼ cup) roasted peanuts

Place the prepared papaya in a large mixing bowl. Cut the snake beans into 4 cm (1½ inch) lengths, then blanch them in boiling salted water for 2 minutes. Refresh in iced water, drain and allow to dry. Cut the cherry tomatoes in half and slice the herbs finely, reserving some whole herbs for garnish.

Put the snake beans, tomatoes and herbs in the bowl with the papaya. Add the dressing and mix quite vigorously, squeezing the ingredients as you toss the salad. Place the salad in a serving bowl and garnish with the fried shallots, peanuts and reserved herbs.

Note: In Vietnam, women hold the green papaya in one hand and, with a sharp knife in the other, rapidly and repeatedly cut into the fruit; fine shards fall away into a bowl. You can buy a special tool from an Asian supermarket that shreds the papaya beautifully (and safely), or simply slice the papaya very finely, then cut it into long thin strips.

LIME & CHILLI DRESSING MAKES 250 ML (9 FL OZ/1 CUP)

1 garlic clove
1 bird's eye chilli
50 g (1¾ oz) palm sugar (jaggery), grated
2½ tablespoons light soy sauce

100 ml (3½ fl oz) lime juice
2 teaspoons chilli oil
25 ml (1 fl oz) vegetable oil
1 tablespoon chopped coriander (cilantro)

Pound the garlic and chilli into a fine paste using a mortar and pestle. Add the palm sugar and continue to pound the ingredients together. Add the soy sauce and stir well until the sugar dissolves, then add the remaining ingredients, stirring well to combine. This dressing is best used fresh, but can be kept for up to 2 days in the fridge.

STEAMED ASIAN GREENS WITH TAMARI SAUCE & FRIED SHALLOTS

6 SERVES / SIDE DISH

600 g (1 lb 5 oz) mixed Asian greens,
    such as bok choy (pak choy), Chinese
    broccoli (gai larn) and choy sum
2½ tablespoons tamari sauce
100 ml (3½ fl oz) vegetable stock or water
1 teaspoon potato starch

40 g (1½ oz/½ cup) fried Asian shallots
40 g (1½ oz/¼ cup) peanuts, chopped
1 handful of coriander (cilantro) leaves
2 bird's eye chillies, finely sliced
1 teaspoon organic toasted sesame oil

Trim the Asian greens and cut into 5 cm (2 inch) lengths. Wash in a large bowl, then drain and set aside. Place a bamboo steaming basket over a large saucepan of boiling water, add the vegetables and steam until tender but still resistant to the bite.

    Meanwhile, put the tamari and stock in a saucepan and bring to the boil. Mix the potato starch with 1 tablespoon of water, then add it to the tamari sauce. Stir to thicken slightly, then remove from the heat. Place the Asian greens on a platter and spoon over the tamari sauce. Garnish with the shallots, peanuts, coriander and chilli, and spoon the sesame oil over the top.

OVEN-ROASTED ONIONS WITH GARLIC & WHITE WINE

4 SERVES / SIDE DISH

8 small onions, unpeeled
40 g (1½ oz) butter
12 garlic cloves, unpeeled

200 ml (7 fl oz) white wine
1 bay leaf
chopped parsley, to serve

Preheat the oven to 160°C (315°F/Gas 2–3). Lay the onion on a chopping board with the root end of the onion facing the bottom of the board. Now cut it in half vertically through the middle, leaving the majority of skin on the onion. Repeat for all the onions.

    Place an ovenproof frying pan over medium heat. Melt the butter in the pan, then add the onions, cut side down. Cook for about 5 minutes, or until the onions start to caramelise. Add the garlic cloves, wine and bay leaf, cover loosely with foil, then place in the oven and cook for 20 minutes, or until the onions are soft. To serve, remove the onion skins, season with sea salt and freshly ground black pepper and sprinkle with the parsley.

MOST CULTIVATED AND ASIAN MUSHROOMS
ARE AVAILABLE YEAR-ROUND, ALTHOUGH
WILD MUSHROOMS ARE GENERALLY ONLY
IN SEASON DURING AUTUMN AND WINTER.
THIS DISH WILL WORK WELL WITH ANY
COMBINATION OF MUSHROOMS — TRY
VARIETIES SUCH AS SLIPPERY JACKS,
CHANTERELLES AND PINE MUSHROOMS.

SAUTÉED MUSHROOMS WITH FRENCH SHALLOTS & OREGANO

4 SERVES / SIDE DISH

200 g (7 oz) shiitake mushrooms
200 g (7 oz) shimeji mushrooms
200 g (7 oz) oyster mushrooms
4 tablespoons olive oil

100 g (3½ oz) French shallots, finely sliced
2 garlic cloves, finely chopped
2 tablespoons chopped oregano
1 tablespoon finely grated lemon zest

Trim the mushrooms and wipe with a damp cloth. Place a frying pan over medium–high heat, add the olive oil and then the mushrooms, and toss the pan to distribute the mushrooms. Reduce the heat to medium and add the shallots and garlic. Cook for 5 minutes, tossing the pan occasionally so the ingredients cook evenly. Add the oregano and lemon zest and cook for a further 2 minutes. Season with sea salt and freshly ground black pepper, and serve.

BORLOTTI BEANS WITH HARD HERBS & OLIVE OIL

6 SERVES / SIDE DISH

4 garlic cloves, chopped
100 ml (3½ fl oz) olive oil
1 celery stalk, cut into 5 mm (¼ inch) dice
1 carrot, cut into 5 mm (¼ inch) dice
1 onion, cut into 5 mm (¼ inch) dice

600 g (1 lb 5 oz) shelled fresh borlotti beans
1 litre (35 fl oz/4 cups) vegetable stock
10 g (¼ oz/¼ cup) mixed roughly chopped
   hard herbs, such as rosemary, thyme
   and oregano

Put the garlic in a saucepan over medium heat with 4 tablespoons of the olive oil. Fry for 2 minutes, then add the celery, carrot and onion. Cook for 5 minutes, then add the borlotti beans and stir to combine. Add the stock and bring it to the boil, then reduce the heat, cover the surface with non-stick baking paper and simmer for 30 minutes, stirring occasionally. The beans are cooked when they are tender but remain firm to the bite.

Stir in the herbs and cook for another 2 minutes. Season with sea salt and freshly ground black pepper, then stir in the remaining olive oil. The beans can be served hot or cold.

SIMPLE AND DELICIOUS DISHES ARE ACHIEVED BY COMBINING
INGREDIENTS THAT ARE AT THEIR BEST AT THE SAME TIME OF THE
SEASON. THIS IS PERFECTLY DEMONSTRATED IN THIS TRADITIONAL
MIDDLE EASTERN SALAD OF CARROTS AND ORANGES, BOTH OF
WHICH ARE AT THEIR PEAK IN AUTUMN. THE ADDITION OF SHERRY
VINEGAR IS NOT TRADITIONAL, BUT IS SOMETHING THAT I LIKE TO
DO TO GIVE THE SALAD A TOUCH OF ACIDITY.

CARROT, ORANGE & BLACKCURRANT SALAD

6 SERVES / SIDE DISH

100 g (3½ oz) dried blackcurrants
2 navel oranges
600 g (1 lb 5 oz) grated carrot (4 carrots)
1 handful of mint leaves, roughly chopped

1 long red chilli, finely sliced (seeded
   if you prefer)
3 tablespoons sherry vinegar
125 ml (4 fl oz/½ cup) olive oil

Soak the currants in boiling water for 5 minutes. Drain and allow to cool.

Cut the top and bottom off the oranges, then remove the rest of the skin by following the contour of the orange, working from top to bottom with your knife. Work around the orange until all the skin and pith have been removed. To segment the orange, lay it on its side and slice in between the white pith towards the middle of the orange until all the flesh has been removed. Reserve the segments, along with any juice, and place in a bowl. Repeat for the second orange.

Combine the grated carrot, mint, chilli, currants and orange segments and juice in a bowl. Add the vinegar and olive oil and mix well. Season to taste with sea salt and freshly ground black pepper, and serve.

MY THREE-MUSHROOM BROTH

4 SERVES / STARTER

40 g (1½ oz) butter, softened
1 tablespoon olive oil
4 spring onions (scallions)
200 g (7 oz) pine mushrooms, finely sliced
2 garlic cloves, finely chopped
200 g (7 oz) portobello mushrooms,
    trimmed

200 g (7 oz) enoki mushrooms,
    trimmed
1 litre (35 fl oz/4 cups) vegetable stock
1 long red chilli, finely sliced
50 g (1¾ oz/½ cup) grated parmesan
    cheese

Mix the butter and olive oil together in a small bowl. Trim and clean the spring onions and cut off the lower white part of each stem. Bash the white part into a paste in a mortar and pestle. Finely slice the green part of the spring onion and set aside.

Place a frying pan over medium–high heat and add one-third of the butter and olive oil. When it is sizzling, add the pine mushrooms and one-third of the garlic. Toss and cook the mushrooms until they are coloured around the edges, then tip them into a large saucepan. Repeat this process in two more batches with the portobello and enoki mushrooms, using the remaining butter, olive oil and garlic. Tip the cooked mushrooms into the saucepan.

Add the spring onion paste to the saucepan along with the stock. Place on the stovetop and bring to a rapid boil. Season with sea salt and freshly ground black pepper, then ladle the soup into four bowls. Garnish with the finely sliced spring onion, chilli and parmesan.

STEAMED BUTTER LETTUCE LEAVES STUFFED WITH SAUTÉED MUSHROOMS, POTATO & SPINACH

4-6 SERVES / STARTER

250 g (9 oz) whole potato, unpeeled
    (1 or 2 depending on size)
2 butter lettuces
250 g (9 oz) English spinach, trimmed
250 g (9 oz) mixed mushrooms,
    trimmed

4 tablespoons olive oil
1 onion, diced
2 garlic cloves, finely chopped
1 teaspoon chopped thyme
¼ teaspoon ground nutmeg
100 g (3½ oz) ricotta cheese

Put the potato in a small saucepan, cover with cold water and bring to the boil. Reduce the heat and gently simmer until the potato is tender. Drain and cool slightly, then peel off the skin and cut the potato into 1 cm (½ inch) dice. Set aside.

Separate the lettuce leaves, wash thoroughly, then place them in a colander to dry, or use a salad spinner. Sort through the leaves and separate the larger leaves from the smaller ones (you will need about 35 large leaves, which will be used to wrap up the filling). Wash, dry and roughly chop the spinach and small lettuce leaves.

Wipe the mushrooms clean with a damp cloth, then slice them. Place a frying pan over medium heat, add the olive oil, onion and garlic and cook until just coloured. Increase the heat, add the mushrooms and thyme and cook the mushrooms until the moisture evaporates. Add the chopped spinach and lettuce and cook until it starts to wilt, then add the potato. Continue to cook until the potato has absorbed most of the liquid from the spinach and lettuce, then remove the pan from the heat. Season with the nutmeg, and sea salt and freshly ground black pepper to taste. Stir through the ricotta cheese and allow the mixture to cool.

Lay the whole lettuce leaves on a chopping board and spoon about 1 tablespoon of the cooled filling onto the leaf. Fold in the sides of the leaf and then roll the leaf up to make a neat parcel. Repeat the process until you have used all the filling mixture.

Place a bamboo steaming basket over a large pan of boiling water. Working in batches, steam the parcels for 3 minutes, then remove from the basket and serve.

ASIAN MUSHROOMS & LOTUS ROOT STIR-FRIED WITH GINGER

4 SERVES / SIDE DISH

100 g (3½ oz) fresh lotus root (see Note)
1 tablespoon peanut oil
2 teaspoons finely grated ginger
1 teaspoon finely chopped garlic
100 g (3½ oz) enoki mushrooms
100 g (3½ oz) oyster mushrooms
100 g (3½ oz) shiitake mushrooms

1½ tablespoons oyster sauce
1 teaspoon sugar
a pinch of sea salt
2 spring onions (scallions), finely sliced on the diagonal
1 long red chilli, finely sliced on the diagonal

Peel the lotus root and slice into 3 mm (⅛ inch) slices. Cook the lotus root in boiling salted water for 5–8 minutes, or until tender, then refresh in iced water. Drain and allow it to dry.

Heat a wok over high heat (just before smoking), then add the peanut oil, ginger, garlic and mushrooms in quick succession, and toss well to combine the flavours. Add the lotus root, then the oyster sauce, sugar and sea salt. Toss for 2–3 minutes until the lotus root is heated through. Add the spring onion and chilli and toss to combine, then serve.

Note: Lotus root is available fresh or frozen from Asian supermarkets. If you are buying it fresh, choose the thinner pieces as they are younger and more tender.

STEAMED CHINESE BROCCOLI WITH OYSTER & PLUM SAUCE

4 SERVES / SIDE DISH

125 ml (4 fl oz/½ cup) oyster sauce
3 tablespoons plum sauce
2 teaspoons sugar

a pinch of sea salt
3 tablespoons hot water
2 bunches of Chinese broccoli (gai larn)

To make a sauce, combine the oyster sauce, plum sauce, sugar, salt and hot water in a bowl.

Trim and discard the first 1 cm (½ inch) from the bottom of the Chinese broccoli, then cut into 5 cm (2 inch) lengths. Place in a steamer over a large saucepan of boiling water and steam for 3 minutes. Drain the excess moisture from the broccoli, then arrange it on a serving platter. Dress with a liberal amount of the oyster and plum sauce.

CARAMELISED FENNEL, VALENCIA ORANGE, TOMATO & OLIVE RAGOUT

6 SERVES / SIDE DISH

2 fennel bulbs, about 600 g (1 lb 5 oz) each
4 valencia oranges
100 ml (3½ fl oz) olive oil
2½ tablespoons white wine vinegar

200 g (7 oz) cherry tomatoes, halved
100 g (3½ oz) black olives
1 handful of parsley, roughly chopped

Trim the fennel tops, reserving any smaller stems. Trim off the bottom core of the fennel bulb, then slice it in half. Continue to slice the bulb in half until you have eight pieces about 1.5 cm (⅝ inch) wide at the thickest edge. Repeat for the second fennel bulb.

Cut the top and bottom off two of the oranges, then remove the rest of the skin by following the contour of the orange, working from top to bottom, with your knife. Work around the orange until all the skin and pith have been removed. To segment the orange, lay it on its side and slice in between the white pith towards the middle of the orange until all the flesh has been removed. Reserve the segments and place in a bowl. Squeeze the juice from the remaining two oranges, reserving the juice.

To cook the fennel, heat a large frying pan over medium heat and add the olive oil. When the oil is hot but not smoking, add the fennel and fennel stems, taking care to lay the pieces flat in the pan, without overcrowding. You may have to fry the fennel in batches. Cook for 4 minutes, or until the fennel takes on a nice caramel colour, then turn and caramelise the other side. Add the reserved orange juice and vinegar and continue to cook until the liquid has reduced by a third. Add the tomatoes, olives and orange segments and cook for another 5 minutes. Remove the pan from the heat and stir through the parsley. Season with sea salt and freshly ground black pepper, and serve. This dish can be served hot or cold.

CHINESE CABBAGE, FRIED NOODLE & PEANUT SALAD

6 SERVES / MAIN OR SIDE DISH

2 tablespoons chopped garlic
125 ml (4 fl oz/½ cup) vegetable oil
1 kg (2 lb 4 oz) Chinese cabbage (wongbok)
½ red onion, finely sliced
1 large handful of perilla leaves, finely
  sliced
1 handful of mint leaves, finely sliced
1 large handful of Vietnamese mint leaves,
  finely sliced

100 g (3½ oz) chopped roasted peanuts
90 g (3¼ oz) fried egg noodles (see Note)

DRESSING
3 tablespoons tamari sauce
2 tablespoons rice vinegar
2 tablespoons water
2 teaspoons sesame oil
1 tablespoon caster (superfine) sugar

To make the dressing, combine all the dressing ingredients in a small bowl, stirring until the sugar dissolves, and set aside.

Put the garlic and oil in a small saucepan over medium heat. Gently fry the garlic until it is golden brown (be careful not to overcook it). Strain the garlic through a metal sieve and drain on paper towel.

Slice the cabbage as finely as you can, wash it well, then place in a colander and leave to dry. Place the cabbage in a mixing bowl with the onion, herbs, fried garlic and roasted peanuts. Add the dressing to the salad and mix well. Break the fried noodles over the top of the salad, gently mix and serve.

Note: You can buy fried egg noodles from Asian supermarkets or you can make them easily by deep-frying fresh egg noodles. Make sure the noodles are dry and then deep-fry at 180°C (350°F) until crisp and golden. If you don't have a thermometer, heat some vegetable oil in a large heavy-based saucepan until a cube of bread dropped into the oil turns golden brown in 15 seconds; at this stage the oil is at the correct temperature.

ROASTED BEETROOT

4 SERVES / SIDE DISH

1 bunch beetroot (about 500 g/1 lb 2 oz
    or 4 beetroot)
6 garlic cloves, unpeeled
8–10 thyme sprigs

extra virgin olive oil
310 g (11 oz/1 cup) rock salt
8 cm (3¼ inch) piece of horseradish,
    peeled and grated

Preheat the oven to 180°C (350°F/Gas 4). Cut the leaves from the beetroot, leaving about 2 cm (¾ inch) of stalk above the bulb. If you cut the skin, the colour and natural juices will run from the beetroot, decreasing the intensity of the flavour. Scrub the beetroot thoroughly in cold water, dry and place in a mixing bowl with the garlic cloves and thyme sprigs. Add a good drizzle of extra virgin olive oil to the bowl and mix to coat the beetroot and garlic well.

Put the rock salt in a roasting tray and place the beetroot, garlic and thyme on top. The rock salt will help prevent the bottom of the beetroot from burning. Cover loosely with foil and roast for 30 minutes. Remove the foil and garlic, and set the garlic aside. Turn the beetroot over, cover with the foil and continue roasting for a further 30 minutes. After this time, check to see if the beetroot are soft by piercing them with a skewer — the skewer should easily slip through the beetroot.

When the beetroot are cool enough to handle, gently peel off the skin, cut them into quarters and then place onto a serving dish. Squeeze the garlic flesh from the cloves over the beetroot, add a splash of olive oil and dress the beetroot with the horseradish. Season with sea salt and freshly ground black pepper.

ROASTED BEETROOT SALAD WITH WITLOF, WALNUTS, CHIVE & YOGHURT DRESSING

4 SERVES / SIDE DISH

20 g (¾ oz) butter
50 g (1¾ oz/½ cup) walnut halves
1 bunch beetroot (about 500 g/1 lb 2 oz
    or 4 beetroot), roasted (page 66)
3 heads of witlof
2 spring onions (scallions)

CHIVE AND YOGHURT DRESSING
finely grated zest and juice of ½ orange
2 tablespoons sherry vinegar
2 tablespoons extra virgin olive oil
100 g (3½ oz) natural Greek yoghurt
½ bunch of chives, finely chopped

Place a frying pan over medium heat and add the butter. When the butter has melted, add the walnuts and fry until golden brown, then remove and drain on paper towel. Allow to cool.

Slice the roasted beetroot into 2 cm (¾ inch) wedges. Separate the leaves of the witlof, then wash and dry them. Slice the spring onion into 2 cm (¾ inch) lengths on the diagonal.

To make the chive and yoghurt dressing, put the orange zest and juice and vinegar in a bowl. Add the olive oil and yoghurt and whisk to combine. Season with sea salt and freshly ground black pepper, then fold through the chives.

Build the salad on a platter by placing the beetroot down first, followed by the witlof leaves, spring onion slices and walnuts. Spoon the dressing evenly over the ingredients. If you like, you can serve the salad topped with soft poached biodynamic eggs.

CELERIAC REMOULADE

4 SERVES / SIDE DISH

2 celeriac
2 tablespoons salted capers, rinsed
2 tablespoons chopped parsley

2 tablespoons chopped tarragon
100 g (3½ oz) garlic mayonnaise
  (recipe below)

Trim and peel the celeriac and coarsely grate it to give 750 g (1 lb 10 oz). Put the celeriac in a bowl with the capers, parsley, tarragon and garlic mayonnaise. Season with sea salt and freshly ground black pepper and mix well.

GARLIC MAYONNAISE MAKES 250 G (9 OZ/1 CUP)

3 garlic cloves
2 egg yolks
1 tablespoon dijon mustard
1 tablespoon lemon juice

¼ teaspoon sea salt
¼ teaspoon freshly ground black pepper
200 ml (7 fl oz) vegetable oil
2½ tablespoons olive oil

Bash the garlic cloves into a paste in a mortar and pestle. Transfer the garlic to a stainless-steel bowl with the egg yolks, mustard, lemon juice, salt and pepper. Mix these ingredients well. Combine the vegetable and olive oils, then slowly whisk the oil into the egg base, a few drops at a time, until you have added about 50 ml (1¾ fl oz) of oil. Add the remaining oil in a constant stream, whisking until the mayonnaise is complete.

DEEP-FRIED OKRA WITH TOMATO & CHILLI JAM

6 SERVES / SIDE DISH

500 g (1 lb 2 oz) okra
2 litres (70 fl oz/8 cups) vegetable oil,
    for deep-frying
2 egg whites
180 g (6¼ oz/1 cup) potato starch

TOMATO AND CHILLI JAM
500 g (1 lb 2 oz) vine-ripened tomatoes
100 ml (3½ fl oz) peanut oil

1 red onion, finely diced
1 tablespoon finely chopped garlic
5 long red chillies, seeded and finely
    chopped
2 bird's eye chillies, seeded and finely
    chopped
2 tablespoons grated galangal
250 g (9 oz) palm sugar (jaggery), grated
60 g (2¼ oz/¼ cup) tamarind purée

Wash the okra thoroughly under cold running water, then dry with a kitchen cloth.

To make the tomato and chilli jam, first peel the tomatoes. Score a cross in the base of each tomato with a sharp knife. Put the tomatoes in a heatproof bowl and cover with boiling water. Leave for 30–60 seconds, then refresh in a bowl of iced water. Peel the skin away from the cross and discard it. Cut into quarters, then finely chop.

Place a frying pan over medium heat, add the peanut oil and, when hot, add the onion and garlic. Gently fry until the garlic just starts to colour and the onion softens, then add the chilli and galangal and fry for 2 minutes. Add the palm sugar and stir gently until it melts. Stir through the tomato, then bring the jam to a simmer. Continue to cook and reduce the jam until it thickens, stirring occasionally so that it doesn't stick to the base of the pan. To finish, add the tamarind purée and season to taste with sea salt. Cool to room temperature.

Pour the oil into a large heavy-based saucepan or deep-fryer and heat to 180°C (350°F), or until a cube of bread dropped into the oil turns golden brown in 15 seconds. Lightly whisk the egg whites in a bowl, then fold through all of the okra.

Mix half the potato starch with the okra in the bowl. Add more potato starch if necessary, so that the okra is well coated. Working in small batches, fry the okra in the oil until they are crisp, then remove and drain on paper towel. Serve the okra with the tomato and chilli jam.

A SIMPLE ACT CAN MAKE A BIG IMPRESSION

WHEN I SHOP FOR FRESH PRODUCE AT THE MARKET, I LIKE TO TAKE MY SIX-YEAR-OLD DAUGHTER, MIA, WITH ME. I'VE BEEN DOING THIS SINCE SHE WAS THREE.

Originally I thought it would be a fun father–daughter thing to do, but it didn't take me long to realise that by doing this I was actually getting her excited about food. Now she is so accustomed to the experience and enjoys the hustle and bustle, sights and smells of an open-air market. Walking through the market looking at freshly harvested fruit and vegetables displayed on trestle tables is a timeless experience — this is shopping the way it has been done for hundreds of years. To touch and hold raw produce in your hands is a simple yet rewarding pleasure. It provides the link back to the soil in which the produce was grown. There is no better way to shop; sharing time with my daughter, while instilling in her my love of food, fills me with hope — hope that sustainable and nourishing food is safe in innocent hands.

KIPFLER POTATOES WITH GARLIC, LEMON THYME & CHILLI

4 SERVES / SIDE DISH

750 g (1 lb 10 oz) small kipfler potatoes,
  unpeeled
1 tablespoon salt
1 garlic bulb

150 ml (5 fl oz) olive oil
½ bunch of lemon thyme
2 long red chillies, finely sliced

Put the potatoes in a saucepan and cover with cold water. Add the salt, then place the pan over high heat and bring to the boil. Boil rapidly for 8 minutes, then remove from the heat and drain. Cut the potatoes in half lengthways and allow the skins to dry.

Place a kitchen cloth over the garlic bulb and give it a good whack with a meat mallet. This should separate the cloves, leaving most of the skin on the garlic (this will protect the garlic as it fries). Place a frying pan over medium heat and add the olive oil. Add the potatoes and garlic and gently bring the heat up so they start to fry. Cook slowly, stirring occasionally for about 10 minutes, or until the potatoes are golden and the garlic is soft. Add the lemon thyme and chilli and cook for 5 minutes. Season with sea salt and freshly ground black pepper.

KOHLRABI PURÉE

4 SERVES / SIDE DISH

2 kohlrabi, peeled and cut into quarters
1 small onion, cut into quarters
2 garlic cloves, peeled
2 cloves
1 bay leaf

cold milk, to cover
275 g (9¾ oz) thick (double/heavy) cream
  (45% fat or higher)
1 tablespoon grated fresh horseradish
1 tablespoon wholegrain mustard

Place the kohlrabi, onion, garlic cloves, cloves and bay leaves in a saucepan and cover with the milk. Place the pan over high heat, bring to just before boiling point, then turn the heat down and simmer for about 20 minutes, or until the kohlrabi are soft. Add the cream and continue to simmer until the cream has become quite thick. Remove the cloves and bay leaf, then transfer the contents to a blender. Add the horseradish and mustard and purée the mixture until smooth. Season with sea salt and freshly ground black pepper.

BRUSSELS SPROUTS WITH GARLIC & SPRING ONION

6 SERVES / SIDE DISH

750 g (1 lb 10 oz) brussels sprouts
1 bunch of spring onions (scallions)
4 tablespoons olive oil
20 g (¾ oz) butter

2 garlic cloves, finely chopped
500 ml (17 fl oz/2 cups) vegetable stock
1 tablespoon soft brown sugar

Slice the brussels sprouts in half, wash thoroughly, then tip them into a colander and allow to dry. Slice the white part of the spring onions into 4 cm (1½ inch) lengths and cut half of the remaining green part diagonally to be used as garnish, and set aside.

Place a large frying pan over medium heat, add half the olive oil, the butter and garlic and cook for 1 minute. Add the brussels sprouts in two batches, cut side down, and cook until golden brown. Return all the brussels sprouts to the pan with the white part of the spring onion, stock and sugar. Bring to the boil, then reduce the heat and simmer for 10 minutes until tender. Add the remaining oil and season to taste. Garnish with the spring onion greens.

ROASTED PUMPKIN WITH PINE NUTS & SAGE BURNT BUTTER

6 SERVES / SIDE DISH

750 g (1 lb 10 oz) thin-skinned pumpkin
 (winter squash) such as kent, cut into
 3 cm (1¼ inch) squares
4 garlic cloves, roughly chopped

2½ tablespoons olive oil
50 g (1¾ oz/⅓ cup) pine nuts
100 g (3½ oz) unsalted butter
½ bunch of sage, picked

Preheat the oven to 200°C (400°F/Gas 6). Put the pumpkin in a bowl with the garlic and olive oil, season, and mix well. Tip into a roasting tin and roast for 30 minutes, or until the pumpkin is golden brown and tender. Arrange the pumpkin on a serving platter or in a bowl.

Fry the pine nuts in the butter over medium heat, stirring occasionally until they start to colour, then add the sage. Stir until the sage is crisp and the pine nuts are golden brown. The butter solids at this stage will be rich and dark. Pour the sage butter over the pumpkin.

BROWN LENTIL CASSEROLE WITH VEGETABLES & THYME

4 SERVES / MAIN

370 g (13 oz/2 cups) brown lentils
20 g (¾ oz) butter
2 tablespoons olive oil
2 celery stalks, finely chopped
2 carrots, finely chopped
1 leek, white part only, washed and finely
   chopped

5–6 thyme sprigs
500 ml (17 fl oz/2 cups) vegetable stock
1 garlic clove, peeled
2 bay leaves
1 large handful of parsley leaves,
   roughly chopped
½ lemon

Soak the lentils in cold water for 1 hour, then drain. Place the butter, olive oil, celery, carrot and leek into a large saucepan and fry the vegetables until they are soft. Add the thyme and stir the ingredients well to combine. Add the lentils, then pour enough stock into the pan to just cover them. Add the garlic clove and bay leaves and bring everything to the boil, then reduce the heat and simmer gently for about 20 minutes, or until the lentils are cooked.

To serve, season with sea salt and freshly ground black pepper, stir through the parsley and add a squeeze of lemon.

SPICY CHICKPEA & TOMATO CURRY

6 SERVES / MAIN

400 g (14 oz) dried chickpeas, soaked
    in cold water overnight
2 garlic cloves, peeled
1 onion, quartered
100 ml (3½ fl oz) vegetable oil
500 g (1 lb 2 oz) onions, finely sliced
4 garlic cloves, finely chopped
1 lemongrass stem, white part only, finely
    chopped

1 tablespoon Malaysian red curry powder
2 teaspoons ground turmeric
1 teaspoon ground galangal
100 g (3½ oz) palm sugar (jaggery), grated
2 x 400 g (14 oz) tins chopped tomatoes
white pepper
juice of 1 lemon
1 bunch of coriander (cilantro), leaves
    chopped

Strain the chickpeas from the water, then rinse and put in a large saucepan. Cover with cold
water and bring to the boil. Add the garlic cloves and quartered onion and cook for about
1 hour, or until the chickpeas are tender. Drain and set aside.

    Meanwhile, prepare the curry. Place a large saucepan over medium heat, add the oil
and sliced onions and stir constantly until the onions start to break down and become
translucent. Add the chopped garlic and lemongrass and stir to combine the ingredients.
Continue to cook very slowly until the onions caramelise. Add the curry powder, turmeric,
galangal and palm sugar, stirring the curry until the palm sugar melts, then add the tomatoes.
Bring everything to the boil, then reduce the heat and simmer for 10 minutes. Add the
chickpeas and cook for another 10 minutes. To serve, season with sea salt, white pepper and
lemon juice, then stir through the coriander leaves.

WINTER VEGETABLE SOUP

6 SERVES / STARTER

400 g (14 oz) dried borlotti beans, soaked
   in cold water overnight
1 onion, quartered
2 garlic cloves, peeled
1 bay leaf
½ bunch of thyme, leaves picked
2 turnips, cut into 1 cm (½ inch) dice

2 swedes (rutabagas), cut into 1 cm
   (½ inch) dice
½ savoy cabbage, roughly shredded
2 carrots, cut into 1 cm (½ inch) dice
3 celery stalks, roughly diced
4 tablespoons olive oil
½ lemon

Drain the borlotti beans, rinse and place in a large saucepan. Cover with 3 litres (105 fl oz/
12 cups) of water, then add the onion, garlic cloves, bay leaf and thyme and bring to the boil.
Reduce the heat and simmer for 1 hour, or until the beans are just tender. Remove half the
beans and place in a food processor with a little of the cooking liquid. Blend into a purée.

Place all the remaining winter vegetables into the pan and cook until tender — about
15–20 minutes. To serve, stir the borlotti bean purée and olive oil through the soup, add
a good squeeze of lemon, and season with sea salt and freshly ground black pepper.

SUGAR-&-SPICED KALE

4 SERVES / SIDE DISH

2 heads of green kale
2 heads of red kale
2 tablespoons olive oil
1 onion, finely sliced
125 ml (4 fl oz/½ cup) cider vinegar
125 ml (4 fl oz/½ cup) port

55 g (2 oz/¼ cup firmly packed) soft brown
   sugar
60 g (2¼ oz/½ cup) sultanas
½ cinnamon stick
1 fresh bay leaf

Trim off the bottom of the green and red kale, then finely slice them. Heat the olive oil in a
large stockpot over medium heat. Add the kale and onion and cook for 10 minutes, stirring
occasionally. Add the vinegar, port, brown sugar, sultanas, cinnamon and bay leaf, and bring
to the boil. Reduce the heat, cover the pot and simmer for about 1 hour, stirring occasionally,
until the kale is soft. Season with sea salt and freshly ground black pepper. This dish goes
sensationally well with the barbecued butterflied lamb leg on page 202.

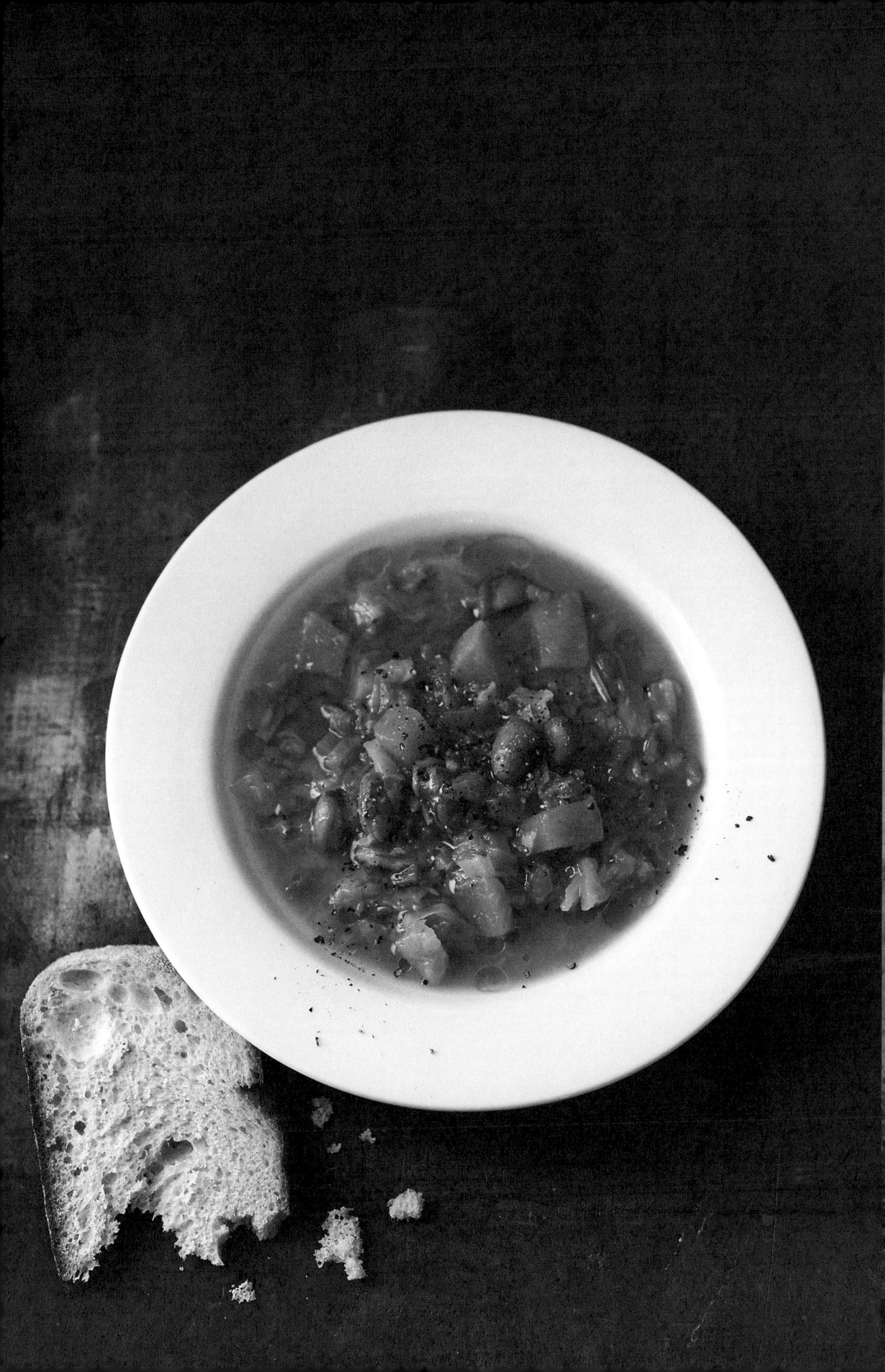

ROAST VEGETABLE SALAD WITH SOFT HERBS & BALSAMIC VINEGAR

6 SERVES / SIDE DISH

3 potatoes
2 carrots
1 large swede (rutabaga)
3 turnips
1 sweet potato
6 small onions, peeled

1 garlic bulb
2 tablespoons olive oil, plus extra,
   to drizzle
1 large handful of basil, roughly chopped
1 small handful of parsley, roughly chopped
balsamic vinegar

Preheat the oven to 180°C (350°F/Gas 4). Cut the potatoes, carrots, swede, turnips and sweet potato into pieces about 5 x 3 cm (2 x 1¼ inches) in size. Place the potato into a microwave-safe container with 2 tablespoons of water, then cover and cook for 3 minutes on high, or until almost soft. Put the potato in a mixing bowl with all the vegetables, including the onions and garlic bulb. Pour the olive oil over them and mix to evenly coat in the oil. Place in roasting tins, allowing a small space between each vegetable, and roast for about 40 minutes, or until the vegetables are well coloured and soft on the inside.

Tip into a large bowl and squeeze the garlic from the skins over the top, add the herbs and drizzle with a generous amount of balsamic vinegar and olive oil. Season with sea salt and freshly ground black pepper, then arrange on a serving platter. Serve either hot or cold.

JERUSALEM ARTICHOKE PAN-ROASTED WITH BUTTER & SAGE

4 SERVES / SIDE DISH

600 g (1 lb 5 oz) Jerusalem artichokes
70 g (2½ oz) butter
1 tablespoon olive oil

½ bunch of sage, picked
½ lemon

Preheat the oven to 200°C (400°F/Gas 6). Scrub the artichokes under cold running water. Dry well, then halve lengthways. Place an ovenproof frying pan over medium heat and add 50 g (1¾ oz) of the butter and the olive oil. When the butter starts to foam, add the artichokes. Toss to coat in the butter until they begin to colour. Place the pan in the oven and cook for about 15 minutes. The artichokes are cooked when a skewer passes freely through them.

Return the frying pan to the stovetop over medium heat, add the remaining butter and then the sage. Fry the sage until it is crisp and the butter is fragrant. To serve, season with sea salt and freshly ground black pepper, and add a squeeze of lemon.

CAULIFLOWER & GRUYÈRE GRATIN

6 SERVES / SIDE DISH

50 g (1¾ oz) butter
50 g (1¾ oz/⅓ cup) plain (all-purpose)
   flour
500 ml (17 fl oz/2 cups) milk
½ onion, studded with 4 cloves

1 garlic clove, bashed
100 g (3½ oz) gruyère cheese, grated
white pepper
600 g (1 lb 5 oz) cauliflower, cut into florets
1 tablespoon chopped parsley

To make the sauce for the gratin, melt the butter in a saucepan over medium heat, then add the flour and stir to combine. Cook for 2 minutes, but do not colour. Remove from the heat and cool slightly. Vigorously whisk in the milk to prevent lumps forming in the sauce, then add the onion and garlic clove. Place the pan back over the heat and stir until the sauce simmers. Cook for 20 minutes, then remove from the heat. Either pass the sauce through a sieve or spoon the onion and garlic out of the sauce. While the sauce is hot, stir through the cheese and season with salt and white pepper.

Steam the cauliflower until just tender. Put in a gratin dish and cover with the sauce. Place under a hot grill (broiler) and cook until the sauce is golden brown. Garnish with the parsley.

CONTENTS

EAFOOD **87**

SEAFOOD

I LOVE FISHING AND I OWE MY PASSION FOR THIS TREASURED PASTIME TO MY FATHER. DAD IS AN OBSESSED FISHERMAN. AS CHILDREN WE SPENT A LOT OF TIME FISHING AND CAMPING ALONG THE COAST OF NORTHERN NEW SOUTH WALES AND SOUTHEAST QUEENSLAND. A WEEKEND AWAY FISHING WAS SOMETHING WE ALL LOOKED FORWARD TO. MY FATHER ALWAYS DID HIS HOMEWORK BEFOREHAND, AND WOULD STUDY THE PREVIOUS WEEK'S FISHING REPORTS LIKE AN ARMCHAIR PUNTER STUDIES THE FORM GUIDE. THE LOCATION OF PROLIFIC CATCHES, ATMOSPHERIC PRESSURE AND WIND SPEED WERE CAREFULLY NOTED. AN ITEM THAT TOOK PRIDE OF PLACE BESIDE HIS RECLINING ARMCHAIR WAS A RAGGEDY POCKETBOOK EDITION OF THE TIDE CHARTS. THIS INDISPENSABLE BOOK COULD FORECAST WHETHER THE TIDE AND MOON WOULD ALIGN, POTENTIALLY TIPPING THE ODDS OF SUCCESS IN OUR FAVOUR.

A flurry of activity filled the house as the week drew to a close. 'You better get the tent out and check that it is clean and dry,' my dad would warn us. 'Count the poles and the pegs. Are the ropes there? Is the flysheet folded neatly?' Logically we knew that this ritualistic checking of camping gear was completely unnecessary, as we had meticulously packed it away the weekend before — as per our father's instructions.

We all checked our own fishing rods and tackle, as it was 'the responsibility of the fisherman to tend to his own gear'. My fishing rod and reel were always clean; I would wash the salt off them after every fishing trip. I got many years of use out of my first fishing rod. My dad's cane rod, which he's had since he was a teenager, is still in great condition — and he's now 70 years old. 'If you take care of something, it will take care of you,' he always told us. When I think about the state of our environment today, I often think of the wisdom behind my father's words.

Catching a fish to share with one's family gives an amazing sense of satisfaction and I'm sure it accounts for a large part of fishing's popularity. I still find fishing enjoyable, although finding the time these days can be difficult. In the mid-nineties I became totally enamoured with the art of fly-fishing — the thrill of the hunt and a perfectly cast fly almost but not quite outweighs the adrenaline pump of hooking and playing a fish to the riverbank. Most of the fish I catch are rested and revived before being released back into the river. Resting the fish before releasing it increases its chance of survival, but for those that I do keep, their death is swift. Now my appreciation for the art of fishing is quite different to what it was when I was young. Back then, the success of a fishing trip was measured at the end of the day by the weight of the bag slung over my shoulder. As kids we had no concept of bag limits; fish were only released if they were undersize, or Dad would use the small ones for bait when he went fishing for his beloved tailor.

Fishermen have long prized the tailor as a supreme recreational fishing species. Tailor can grow up to 10 kilograms but are usually caught when they're between 750 grams and 1.5 kilograms. July and August was the time when the tailor migrated from the southeastern seaboard of Australia, up along the New South Wales coast and into

Queensland, to the spawning grounds around Fraser Island. Dad always planned our holidays around this migration.

I remember watching Dad and his mate Digger standing side by side on the sea wall, flanked by hundreds of men. When the fish were 'on' it was a blood bath. Visually it was spectacular; men casting fishing lines baited with pilchards into the water, while others wound fish in, lifting them out of the water, up and over the rocks, the silver skin of the fish glistening in the soft light of the sun as it rose from the ocean. Once caught, tailor are 'bled'. You force your fingers into and out of the other side of the fish's gills then you rip its throat open and drain the fish of its blood. This somewhat barbaric practice improves the eating quality of the fish. The scent of oily pilchards was heavy in the air and the frenzied squawks of hundreds of seagulls diving for the bait added to the primal theatre.

I helped carry the hessian bags laden with fish back to the car and when we counted them, there were close to one hundred fish. Fishing and then scaling, gutting and filleting the fish was an activity I enjoyed doing with my father, but I knew instinctively that this intensive level of fishing was unsustainable. The words I used as a boy were more innocent, however. 'Dad, if we keep catching all these fish, there won't be any left in the ocean.'

Mankind has a deplorable history of exploiting the ocean's natural resources. When whales and seals were hunted in the eighteenth century, they stood a chance of eluding their pursuers because of the limitations of the equipment being used. With the onset of the industrial age, fishing vessels were increasingly mechanised; structurally they were stronger and could remain at sea for longer periods of time. Being motorised, the vessels could outpace whales and seals, enabling the total eradication of their pods. With the advent of refrigeration, fishermen could process and freeze fish on board. This ability, combined with man's propensity for greed and exploitation, would see the beginning of the end for many of the world's fisheries.

Today, the odds are precipitously stacked in the commercial fishermen's favour. Huge factory ships, capable of staying at sea for months at a time, work in tandem with smaller fishing vessels. The factory ships, as the name implies, are floating seafood processing factories equipped with amenities to keep a small army of fishermen busy 24 hours a day. The smaller vessels set out to the fishing grounds in the early morning and return later in the day to unload their catch. The seafood is sorted, cleaned, processed and then frozen on board the ship. The commercial fishing fleets have the capability, if left unchecked, to decimate the ocean's wild fish stock.

METHODS OF COMMERCIAL FISHING

Commercial fishermen generally target individual fish species using one of three basic fishing methods. They use nets, baited hooks set on long lines, or traps.

Nets can be trawled behind a fishing vessel, set at a fixed point or drifted across the ocean surface. Set gillnets catch huge numbers of fish indiscriminately, including non-target fish species and ocean mammals, while seafloor trawling is a method of fishing that scoops up everything that passes in front of the net. Gemfish and orange roughy are popular examples of fish caught in nets, and there are serious concerns about the sustainability of these fish.

Long-line fishing is where a fishing line is tied with up to 15 000 hooks. Frozen baitfish are threaded onto the hooks before being drifted across the ocean's surface to catch species such as yellowfin tuna, swordfish and mahi mahi, or horizontally fixed at a set point above the ocean floor to catch snapper, bass grouper or bar rockcod. A similar technique known as drop-line fishing enables fishermen to reach deepwater species because the line is set vertically, secured to the ocean floor by weights. Fish caught by this method are harpuka, bar rockcod and blue eye trevalla. Although long-line fishing methods have minimal impact on the ocean habitat, they still catch fish indiscriminately, as well as sea birds, turtles and protected species of sharks.

Traps are used to catch both fish and crustaceans and cause the least harm to the environment. Fish such as groper, cod and gold band snapper are caught by this method, as are crabs and lobsters.

THE DAMAGING EFFECTS OF SEAFLOOR TRAWLING

Of the three methods used by commercial fishermen the one that inflicts the most damage on the marine ecology is seafloor trawling. As the name suggests, seafloor trawling is a method whereby a dome-shaped net is weighted down and trawled behind a boat along the seafloor. Chains suspended from the net's mouth drag along the ocean floor, arousing bottom-dwelling species off the floor and into the net. This method targets species such as prawns, flounder, sole and bottom-dwelling blue eye trevalla. Unfortunately, protected marine animals such as turtles, rays and sharks also end up in the nets. I use blue eye in the restaurant occasionally, as it is a popular fish, however, I am not a supporter of seafloor trawling, so when I do use blue eye, I insist that it is line caught.

To stop the nets from becoming entangled in coral or rocks, rollers are attached. These rollers are intended to bounce the nets over obstacles, but instead tend to work like steamrollers, flattening everything in their path, damaging the habitat vital for the many small animals that constitute the beginning of the aquatic food chain.

It is possible to minimise the damaging effects of seafloor trawling by persuading fishermen to use nets designed to let non-target species, or bycatch, escape through specially designed chutes, and encouraging fishermen not to target the species that live in areas where they have to use rollers on their nets. We can do this by not buying the seafood caught in these areas. Seafloor trawling over sandy areas has less impact on the environment yet still catches some great eating fish, including flathead, whiting, sole and bream. The fish found in these areas tend to be the more robust and faster breeding species, and although not immune to overfishing they reach sexual maturity quickly, which helps to alleviate some of the fishing pressure.

Other fishing methods, such as lampara and purse seine nets, allow fishermen to more effectively target desired species. By taking advantage of the schooling nature of fish, fishermen can target and encircle entire schools with their nets. Some of the fish caught in Australian waters by this method are bream, whiting and mulloway. The nets cause little harm to the environment and the number of non-target fish inadvertently caught is minimised.

REDUCING BYCATCH

Bycatch can be broken down into two categories: protected species that are accidentally caught, and non-target species that are caught in the nets only to be discarded because they have no commercial value or because the quantity of fish caught exceeds quotas. Internationally, quota systems exist to limit the number of fish caught each year. They seem to be a necessary evil. Once a fisherman has filled their quota, any fish caught over the specified amount must be discarded, regardless of whether they are dead or dying. Fishermen in Australia are also licensed to catch particular fish species. If they inadvertently catch a net full of fish they are not licensed to catch or if the catch exceeds their quota, they have to dump the fish overboard or otherwise they face huge fines.

The Australian Fishery Management Authority recognises the importance of reducing bycatch for the long-term sustainability of all Commonwealth fisheries and is investigating ways to minimise the practice of discarding fish caught in excess of quotas by factoring them into the initial quota. Other methods for reducing bycatch include trials of fishing gear that mitigates the capture of non-target species. The implementation of one strategy aimed at reducing the number of sea birds diving for and eating baited hooks was to simply ask long-line fishermen to avoid setting up their lines in the early morning, when the birds are most active. Let's hope the other measures being investigated to reduce bycatch prove to be this straightforward.

AQUACULTURE — THE POSITIVES AND NEGATIVES

Aquaculture is thought to have originated in China over 4000 years ago. Today the industry supplies approximately one-third of the seafood we consume and its overall contribution to supply is expected to increase to at least 50 per cent by the year 2030. The decline in wild fish populations is not the only factor contributing to the increase in aquaculture production; the now generally accepted health benefits ascribed to a seafood diet have also fuelled demand.

Aquaculture, or fish farming, is the intensive cultivation of marine and freshwater species of fish, crustaceans and molluscs. These creatures are fed a manufactured diet and are grown in an environment that is scientifically monitored and manipulated to facilitate their growth and welfare. In Australia, because of the country's diverse climatic conditions, we are able to farm about sixty different seafood species. Seafood is farmed in coastal intertidal zones, offshore or in purpose-built onshore facilities. The industry is not without its detractors — if mismanaged it can have a significant impact on the environment.

Perhaps the least invasive form of aquaculture is the farming of molluscs. Species such as oysters, scallops and mussels are filter feeders and require pristine waters to thrive. These bivalves filter the phytoplankton and zooplankton from the water and do not need to be artificially fed. Mussels and oysters are generally grown on ropes, in suspension bags or on trays. The ropes and bags are separated at a predetermined distance to allow mammals such as dolphins to pass through the farming operation with minimal chance of becoming entangled.

Marine fish can be raised in cages positioned several kilometres offshore. The cages are stocked with fish that have been bred in land-based hatcheries from captive populations, or with fish that have been ranched or rounded up from wild populations and herded into the cages to be fattened for market.

Hatchery-bred fish are produced from eggs that are manually harvested and then fertilised. The resulting sprats are then grown to a specified size before being transported to the sea cages that are moored in a nearby harbour. Once the fish are deposited into the cages they are slowly towed out to their ocean position. By contrast, ranched fish tend to be the juveniles of large carnivorous pelagic species such as tuna. Spotter planes search for schools of fish, then guide speedboats into position to chase the fish into the open sea cages. The cages are made from netting and are floated on the ocean's surface. The design of the cages varies depending on the species of fish being raised, but generally the net of the cage protrudes above and extends below the ocean's surface, preventing the fish from escaping, while offering protection from predators.

However, sea-cage farming has the potential to cause significant environmental damage. Because the cages are positioned in the ocean it is difficult to contain excess food, medication or waste generated during production. If the nets are not properly maintained, farmed fish can escape and compete with indigenous fish for food and habitat. Disease can also spread quickly through populations of intensively farmed animals, and fish are no exception. Antibiotics are used to control disease outbreaks and these products can leach into the environment and affect wild fish. However, it is possible to farm fish without antibiotics, and hopefully this will become standard practice in the future. At present, if you are concerned about the use of antibiotics, and not everyone is, it is better to assume all farmed fish have been exposed to it. Believe me, if the farmed fish you are about to buy has not had antibiotics you would certainly know about it — this fact would give the producer an enormous advantage over their competitors.

Fish and crustaceans can also be raised in inland ponds or tanks where the environment or ecosystem within the ponds is controlled and monitored. This method of production is thought to be the most environmentally responsible and sustainable. Many species farmed by this method, such as trout, barramundi, Murray cod and yabbies, are omnivorous so their diet is more varied and less reliant on manufactured fish meal. There is no chance of fish escaping to compete with the wild population and although antibiotics can be used during production, disease can be contained and managed.

One important aspect of this production method is the ability to filter and treat any uneaten food and solid waste produced by the fish. The pond water is continually pumped out and filtered before being circulated back through the system. Once the waste is extracted, it is possible to process it into fertiliser for general agricultural use. Although this is possibly the most sustainable form of fish farming, unfortunately there are significant establishment costs, which make it the least attractive form of farming.

With dwindling wild fish stocks, aquaculture would seem the obvious alternative, but not everyone shares this belief. It can be argued that the industry has placed extra pressure on wild fish populations by removing great numbers of baitfish from the marine food chain. Baitfish are caught and manufactured into fish meal and oil, which is then fed to the farm fish population. (Fish meal can be made from the offal and skeletons of fish that are already processed for our consumption, although it is of a lesser quality.) Aquaculture's reliance on baitfish stock has caused opponents to question the industry's sustainability.

At present the increase in demand for fish meal by the aquaculture industry has been mitigated by a decrease in demand for fish meal by the other agricultural industries. The total tonnage of fish caught for fish meal has remained relatively steady over the last decade, however during this time the aquaculture industry has expanded steadily by 4 per cent per annum. I feel there is little prospect of wild caught fish meal production increasing in the future to stay abreast of industry demands.

It is also argued that aquaculture is an inefficient way to grow fish, as the fish consume several kilograms of wild caught baitfish (in the form of fish meal and oil) for every kilogram of weight they gain. This is called the food conversion ratio; it is one of the measures used by livestock producers to judge the profitability of their stock. The less food an animal eats to gain weight the more profitable it is. Some species are more efficient food converters than others, and the conversion ratio varies depending on the species of fish. Although I can appreciate this argument I have never found it completely convincing. Captive fish are protected from predators and don't have to swim far for their next meal; they convert more of the food they consume into body mass. Wild fish are under constant threat from predators and may need to swim great distances in search of their next meal; they would have to consume more food (wild baitfish) to generate the same gain in body mass. Opponents of the aquaculture industry seem to neglect this fact when presenting their argument.

I do, however, concede that alternative sustainable food sources need to be developed in order to secure the future of the aquaculture industry. The industry is working in conjunction with scientists from the Commonwealth Scientific and Industrial Research Organisation (CSIRO), who are developing substitutes for anchovy-based fish meal derived from terrestrial plants and animals. To date, food derived from lupins (a perennial plant that has high-protein seeds) is providing the most promising results.

THE POWER OF THE CONSUMER

It is possible to farm fish and address all of the negative attributes, although the production costs are significantly higher. Are you prepared to pay more for your seafood to cover these costs, which will ultimately benefit you and the environment? This is the question that more and more of us in the developed world will consider in the future.

One inspiring example of a retail store supporting and championing sustainable, organic aquaculture is the American organic food chain, Whole Foods. They have accepted the sustainable seafood challenge and are only stocking wild seafood products that are endorsed by the Marine Stewardship Council — a non-profit organisation that identifies and promotes sustainable seafood — or seafood that is farmed by sustainable and ethical means. The farmed seafood is produced following a strict code of practice and the production facilities are independently audited to ensure the standards are upheld. The producers must minimise the effects fish farming has on the environment, monitor and prevent water pollution and source sustainable food supplies. The fish must be free of antibiotics and there must be complete traceability from the hatchery to the growing and processing facilities. I believe traceability is a key issue and will become standard practice for all primary agriculture and aquaculture in the future.

With good science and animal husbandry it is possible to improve the way farmed seafood is produced. Scientists are working to identify the genes responsible for the commercially favourable characteristics of wild and farmed breeder fish. With this information, producers will be able to selectively breed fish that grow efficiently on alternative food sources and are more disease tolerant. There is a real opportunity for the ethical and sustainable producers to distinguish themselves from the crowd. The challenge for consumers will be to identify who those producers are.

Whole Foods has implemented a traceability program — perhaps the entire seafood industry needs to get on board? Competition for market share should be waged on the individual producer's environmental credentials and not their ability to put the cheapest product on the shelves. We have to be prepared to pay for ethically produced seafood, but in doing so we need to have confidence in the process. The industry needs to be independently audited and the labels on the final product have to contain standardised language so the consumer can differentiate the products.

Whether we choose to enjoy wild caught or farmed seafood, one thing is clear: we all need to appreciate the role we play in the process if we are to conserve seafood resources for future generations. Fishermen and fish farmers respond to the choices consumers make. If we refuse to buy products that are ethically corrupt, they will soon cease to exist. I think sometimes we forget the power we have as customers. Now is the time to collectively exercise our purchasing muscle.

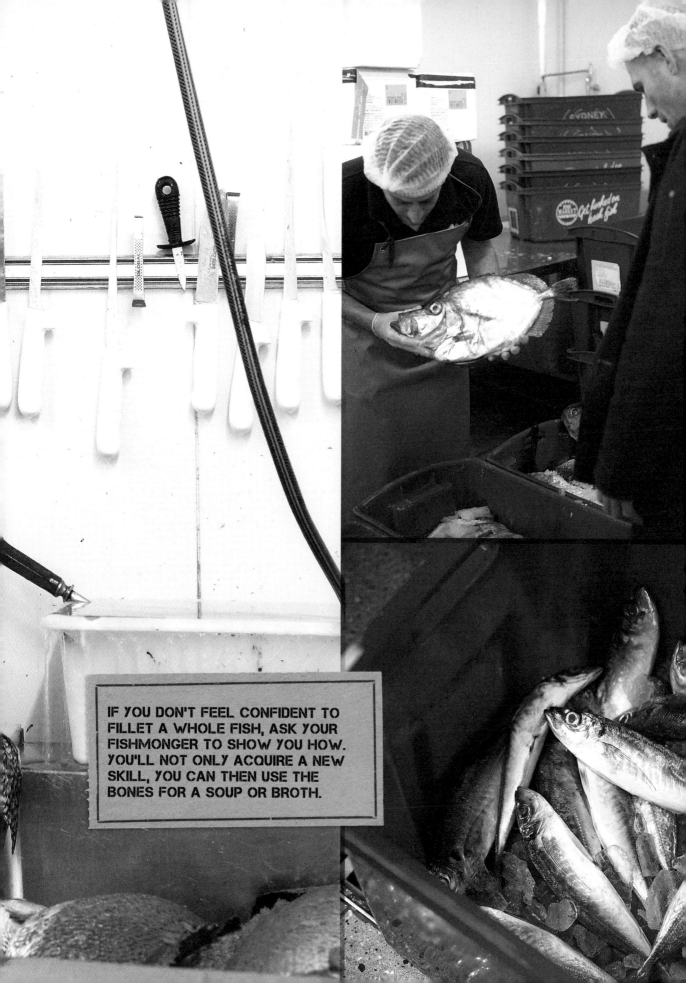

IF YOU DON'T FEEL CONFIDENT TO FILLET A WHOLE FISH, ASK YOUR FISHMONGER TO SHOW YOU HOW. YOU'LL NOT ONLY ACQUIRE A NEW SKILL, YOU CAN THEN USE THE BONES FOR A SOUP OR BROTH.

SQUID SAUTÉED WITH GARLIC, CHILLI & SPRING ONIONS

4 SERVES / STARTER

600 g (1 lb 5 oz) whole squid (or you could use cleaned frozen squid tubes)
100 ml (3½ fl oz) olive oil
2 teaspoons garlic, chopped

2 teaspoons chilli flakes
4 spring onions (scallions), finely sliced on the diagonal (reserve some for garnish)
1 tablespoon lemon or lime juice

To clean the whole squid, lay it on a chopping board, insert your fingers inside the squid and pull the internal organs and legs away from the body. Use a sharp knife to cut the beak from the top of the tentacles, discarding the beak and internal organs. Use your fingers to pull the wings off the squid's body, then proceed to remove all of its skin. Leave the skin on the tentacles. You will now have two pieces — the body and the tentacles. Wash the squid under cold running water and pat dry with paper towel.

Lay the body on a clean chopping board with the top of the squid pointing away from you. Insert the tip of a sharp knife into the top of the fine line that runs along the side of the squid. Cut down to the bottom, then open the body up as you would a book. Working from the top right to the bottom left of the squid, score the squid on a 45 degree angle, making sure you don't cut right through the flesh. Then similarly, work from the top left to the bottom right, to form a diamond pattern of cuts across the squid. Cut the squid vertically in half, then turn the pieces so the top and the bottom face left and right. Cut the body into 2 cm (¾ inch) wide pieces and cut the tentacles into 4 cm (1½ inch) lengths.

Place a large frying pan or wok over high heat and add the olive oil. When the oil is hot but not smoking, add the squid. Move it around the pan with a wooden spoon for 1 minute, then add the garlic, chilli flakes and spring onions. Continue to move the squid around the pan for about 3 minutes until it is cooked. Add the lemon or lime juice and season with sea salt and freshly ground black pepper. Garnish with the reserved spring onion and serve.

SQUID IS PLENTIFUL, REASONABLY INEXPENSIVE AND CAN BE ROASTED, GRILLED, SAUTÉED, OR STUFFED AND STEAMED. YES, IT'S VERY VERSATILE, SO PLEASE TAKE ADVANTAGE OF IT AND EXPERIMENT.

OYSTERS ARE THE ULTIMATE ECO-
FRIENDLY EXTRAVAGANCE. THEY FEED ON
MICROSCOPIC ORGANISMS BY DRAWING
WATER INTO THEIR SHELLS AND FILTERING
THE NUTRIENTS OUT. OYSTERS ARE LIKE
THE CANARIES OF THE SEA; THEY ARE
HIGHLY SENSITIVE TO POLLUTANTS AND
CAN'T SURVIVE IN ANYTHING LESS THAN
PRISTINE WATERS.

SYDNEY ROCK OYSTERS WITH A TAMARIND & LIME DRESSING

4-8 SERVES / STARTER

4 dozen freshly shucked Sydney rock
   oysters (see Note)

DRESSING
2 tablespoons tamarind purée
juice of 1 lime

1 teaspoon very finely chopped ginger
3 tablespoons fish sauce
3 tablespoons rice vinegar
4 tablespoons soft brown sugar
10 large Thai basil leaves, finely sliced

To make the dressing, place all the ingredients, except the basil, in a saucepan with 125 ml (4 fl oz/½ cup) of water and bring to the boil. As soon as the dressing boils and the sugar dissolves, remove the pan from the heat and allow the dressing to cool, then stir through the basil. Arrange the oysters on a platter and spoon 1 teaspoon of dressing onto each oyster.

Note: This recipe makes enough dressing for four dozen oysters. Adjust the quantities to suit the number of people you are serving.

GRILLED WHITING FILLETS WITH GREEN OLIVE TAPENADE

4 SERVES / MAIN

100 g (3½ oz) green olives, pitted
1 garlic clove
4 anchovy fillets
2 tablespoons fresh breadcrumbs

2½ tablespoons extra virgin olive oil
1 small handful of parsley leaves, chopped
800 g (1 lb 12 oz) whiting fillets, skin on,
   pin bones removed

To make the green olive tapenade, place the olive flesh into a food processor with the garlic, anchovies, breadcrumbs and olive oil. Process the ingredients to form a fine paste. Add the parsley and stir to combine.

   Lay the whiting fillets, skin side up, on a baking tray lined with non-stick baking paper. Spread a fine, even layer of tapenade over the skin of the fish. Preheat the grill (broiler) to medium, place the fish under the grill and cook for 5 minutes, or until just cooked through.

YABBIES ARE A GREAT SUSTAINABLE ALTERNATIVE TO PRAWNS. THEY ARE FARMED IN INLAND PONDS, AND ANY WASTE THEY PRODUCE CAN BE FILTERED FROM THE WATER AND USED TO FERTILISE THE LAND.

YABBIES COOKED IN A TOMATO, CHILLI & BLACK PEPPER SAUCE

4 SERVES / STARTER

1 kg (2 lb 4 oz) live yabbies
2½ tablespoons olive oil
2 garlic cloves, finely chopped
1 small onion, finely diced
400 g (14 oz) peeled and chopped tomatoes (see Note), or tinned chopped tomatoes are fine if fresh are not available

2½ tablespoons fish sauce
1 tablespoon caster (superfine) sugar
1 teaspoon sea salt
2 teaspoons minced pickled red chilli
1 teaspoon freshly ground black pepper
2 spring onions (scallions), finely sliced on the diagonal
1 long red chilli, chopped

Put the live yabbies in the freezer; this will humanely prepare them for later use. Place a saucepan over medium heat and add 1 tablespoon of the olive oil. Once the oil is hot, add the garlic and onion and gently fry for about 2 minutes to release the flavours. Add the tomato and stir to combine the flavours. Bring the sauce to the boil, then reduce the heat and simmer gently for 10 minutes. Add the fish sauce, sugar, sea salt, pickled chilli and black pepper, stir to combine, then simmer gently for another 5 minutes. Remove the tomato sauce from the heat and set aside.

Remove the yabbies from the freezer. Preparing the yabbies one at a time, place them on their backs on a chopping board, then cut in half straight down the middle, from head to tail. Place a large frying pan over medium heat and add the remaining olive oil. Once the oil is hot, quickly place all of the yabbies in the pan, flesh side down, and fry for 2 minutes. Add the tomato sauce, stir to combine, and simmer for 4 minutes, or until the yabbies are cooked. Serve the yabbies in a bowl and garnish with the spring onion and chilli.

Note: To peel the tomatoes, score a cross in the base of each tomato. Put the tomatoes in a heatproof bowl and cover with boiling water. Leave for 30–60 seconds, then refresh in a bowl of iced water. Peel the skin away from the cross and discard it, then chop the tomatoes.

BLUE MUSSELS WOK-TOSSED WITH KAFFIR LIME LEAVES, GINGER & GARLIC

4 SERVES / STARTER

1 kg (2 lb 4 oz) blue mussels
1 tablespoon peanut oil
4 cm (1½ inch) piece of young ginger, peeled and finely sliced
2 garlic cloves, finely chopped
2 red Asian shallots, finely sliced
6 kaffir lime (makrut) leaves, very finely sliced

500 ml (17 fl oz/2 cups) vegetable stock
2½ tablespoons fish sauce
1 tablespoon sugar
1 tablespoon potato starch
1 large handful of coriander (cilantro) sprigs
2 limes, cut into wedges

Scrub the mussels under cold running water to remove any dirt or grime. If the hairy beard is attached, pull it off, then rinse again. Discard any broken mussels or open ones that don't close when tapped on the work surface.

Heat a wok or large frying pan over medium heat. Add the peanut oil, ginger, garlic and Asian shallots and fry them to release the flavours. Add the mussels and lime leaves, tossing well to combine the ingredients. Pour the stock and fish sauce over the mussels and increase the heat, then cover with the lid. Lift the lid occasionally and move the mussels around the wok using a charn or wooden spoon. Remove the mussels as they open and put them into a large bowl.

Once all the mussels have opened and have been removed from the wok (discard any mussels that remain closed), reduce the heat to low and add the sugar; taste the sauce and season with sea salt if necessary.

Mix the potato starch with 1 tablespoon of cold water, then add it to the sauce. Add the coriander, then tip the mussels back into the wok and toss to combine. Spoon the mussels into a large serving bowl and serve with the lime wedges on the side.

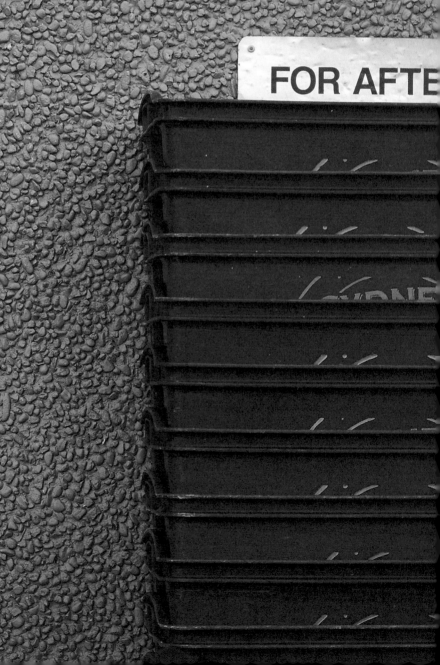

FOR AFTE

SUSTAINABLE SEAFOOD

IT CAN BE COMPLICATED TO SHOP ETHICALLY AND SUSTAINABLY, AS OUR DECISION TO BUY ONE PRODUCT OVER ANOTHER IS GOVERNED BY OUR KNOWLEDGE AT THE TIME.

If we are to buy sustainably produced wild seafood, knowing how it is caught is just as important as knowing which seafood species to buy and which to avoid. Some fish species may be seriously under threat in one area but abundant in another, and it is possible to buy seafood that is considered sustainable only to have it caught in an unsustainable way. It is important to develop a good relationship with your fishmonger; a good seafood supplier is one who is passionate about their produce and appreciates the symbiotic relationship they share with the wild seafood they sell.

BARBECUED SPICED LEMON & ORANGE MARINATED OCTOPUS

4 SERVES / STARTER

1 tablespoon fennel seeds
1 tablespoon cumin seeds
2 tablespoons coriander seeds
4 garlic cloves, chopped
½ bunch of spring onions (scallions), white part only, finely sliced

finely grated zest and juice of 1 lemon
finely grated zest and juice of 1 orange
200 ml (7 fl oz) olive oil
1 medium octopus, about 600 g (1 lb 5 oz)
spring onions (scallions), green part only, finely sliced on the diagonal, to garnish

Dry-roast the spices in a dry frying pan until lightly coloured, then grind to a powder using a mortar and pestle. Place the spices, garlic, spring onion, lemon and orange zests and juices and olive oil into a large bowl.

Remove the head from the octopus, open it up and remove and discard all of the viscera. Wash the head under cold running water, then cut it into eight pieces and set aside. Push the beak from the mouth of the octopus and separate the legs. Cut the legs in half horizontally and place the entire octopus into the marinade. Leave to marinate in the fridge for at least 2 hours, or preferably overnight.

To cook the octopus, preheat your barbecue grill to hot. Remove the octopus from the marinade, place it in a bowl and season generously with sea salt. Make sure you allow some of the marinade to remain on the octopus. Pour the rest of the marinade into a saucepan and place it on the barbecue. Allow the juice to slowly reduce by one-third, then remove the pan from the heat and set aside. Place the octopus on the barbecue and cook for about 3 minutes on each side. Take care not to cook it for too long, as it can become tough — cook until just done in the middle. Place the octopus on a serving platter and drizzle over several spoonfuls of the hot marinade. Garnish with the spring onion.

I RECOMMEND THE AUSTRALIAN SUSTAINABLE SEAFOOD GUIDE AS AN INTRODUCTORY SHOPPING GUIDE FOR SUSTAINABLE SEAFOOD SPECIES. THE GUIDE IS AVAILABLE ONLINE AT WWW.AMCS.ORG.AU OR FOR FURTHER READING, VISIT WWW.MSC.ORG OR WWW.MONTEREYBAYAQUARIUM.ORG.

PAN-FRIED MORWONG FILLET WITH CAPER & PARSLEY BUTTER SAUCE

4 SERVES / MAIN

2 x 600 g (1 lb 5 oz) whole morwong, filleted (this will yield four fillets, about 200 g/7 oz each)
1 tablespoon olive oil
100 g (3½ oz) unsalted butter
2 tablespoons salted capers, rinsed

1 teaspoon finely chopped garlic
1 tablespoon finely chopped French shallot or spring onion (scallion)
1 small handful of parsley leaves, chopped
lemon juice or verjuice, to serve

Lay the fillets, skin side up, on a chopping board. Make three diagonal incisions about 3 mm (⅛ inch) deep through the skin of each fillet. Place a frying pan over medium–high heat. Once the pan is hot, add the olive oil and 20 g (¾ oz) of the butter. When the butter melts and starts to foam, gently place the fish into the pan, skin side down. Lower the heat slightly and cook the fish for about 4 minutes, then turn the fish over, turn off the heat, and continue to cook for 2 minutes. The timing will vary depending on the thickness of the fillets, but with a little practice you will be able to time this to perfection.

Place the fillets on serving plates. Wipe the frying pan clean with paper towel and return the pan to the stove over high heat. Add the remaining butter, and when it foams add the capers, garlic and shallots. Stir until the butter starts to caramelise, then add the parsley and fry until the butter turns golden brown. Remove the pan from the heat and add a squeeze of lemon juice or verjuice. Season the sauce with sea salt and freshly ground black pepper, then spoon evenly over the fish.

> WORLDWIDE, IT IS ESTIMATED THAT 25 PER CENT OF ALL FISH CAUGHT IS CONSIDERED BYCATCH AND IS WASTEFULLY DISCARDED AT SEA. IT IS SWEPT EITHER DEAD OR DYING OFF THE BOAT DECK BACK INTO THE OCEAN.

BARRAMUNDI STEAMED & SERVED WITH A TAMARI & OYSTER SAUCE

2 SERVES / MAIN

1 large barramundi, 600–700 g (1 lb 5 oz
  –1 lb 9 oz)
1 tablespoon peanut oil
¼ teaspoon Chinese five-spice
¼ teaspoon salt
¼ teaspoon white pepper
2 garlic cloves, finely sliced
2 cm (¾ inch) piece of ginger, finely sliced

1 tablespoon oyster sauce
3 tablespoons tamari sauce
½ teaspoon sugar
1 spring onion (scallion), finely sliced
  on the diagonal
1 long red chilli, finely sliced on the
  diagonal

Place a large Chinese metal steamer full of water over high heat and bring to the boil. If you don't have a steamer large enough to accommodate the fish, cut the barramundi into 2 cm (¾ inch) wide cutlets and arrange them in a smaller steamer.

Wash the barramundi inside and out under cold running water, then pat dry with paper towel. Rub 2 teaspoons of the peanut oil over the fish, then season with the five-spice, salt and white pepper. Place the remaining oil on a piece of foil that has been doubled over to strengthen it, then lay the fish on the foil. Scatter the garlic and ginger over the fish, then place it in the steamer over rapidly boiling water for about 18 minutes, or until the fish is firm and flakes easily with a fork. If cooking cutlets, check if they are cooked after 10 minutes.

Meanwhile, combine the oyster sauce, tamari sauce, sugar and 2 tablespoons of hot water, stirring to dissolve the sugar. When the barramundi is cooked, place it on a serving platter and spoon the sauce over the fish. Garnish with the spring onion and chilli, and serve with jasmine rice.

> MOST PEOPLE PREFER THE SWEET, CLEAN FLAVOUR OF EITHER WILD CAUGHT OR FARMED SALTWATER BARRAMUNDI. I TEND TO PREFER THE SUBTLE EARTHINESS OF FRESHWATER BARRAMUNDI. THESE ARE FARMED IN A CONTAINED AQUACULTURE SYSTEM, WHICH CAUSES LESS HARM TO THE ENVIRONMENT.

PAN-FRIED MULLET IN A HERB & GARLIC HOT MARINADE

4 SERVES / MAIN

750 g (1 lb 10 oz) mullet fillets, skin on, deboned

125 ml (4 fl oz/½ cup) olive oil

8 garlic cloves, skin on, crushed with the back of a knife

2 French shallots, finely diced

3 dried long red chillies, roughly chopped

2 tablespoons equal quantities of mixed chopped herbs, such as oregano, thyme and marjoram

1 bay leaf

3 tablespoons verjuice

Trim the mullet fillets into 3 x 9 cm (1¼ x 3½ inch) pieces. Put the fish pieces into a bowl with 2 tablespoons of the olive oil and season with sea salt and freshly ground black pepper. Mix well to coat the fish pieces in the oil and set aside.

Add the remaining olive oil and the garlic cloves to a small saucepan and place over low heat. Cook the garlic until it just starts to colour, then add the shallots and chilli. When the garlic is golden and the shallots are translucent, remove the pan from the heat and set aside.

Place a large cast-iron frying pan over medium heat. When the pan is hot, add a little oil and the mullet pieces, skin side down, and cook until the skin is crisp. Turn the fish over in the pan and immediately turn the heat off.

Put the saucepan of oil, garlic, shallots and chilli back onto high heat and add the herbs and bay leaf. When the herbs start to fry, remove the pan from the heat and carefully add the verjuice. Place the fish on a serving platter (one that will contain the marinade), swirl the hot marinade around in the saucepan and pour evenly over the fish. Allow the fish to marinate for 2 hours before serving. This makes a good picnic dish, served on crusty bread.

FISHERMEN, WORKING IN TANDEM IN TWO BOATS, USUALLY CATCH MULLET JUST OFF THE BEACH IN A PURSE SEINE NET. THIS METHOD OF NETTING FISH IS THE LEAST DEVASTATING ON NON-TARGET SPECIES, RESULTING IN LIMITED BYCATCH.

RAINBOW TROUT COOKED IN YOGHURT WITH INDIAN SPICES

2 SERVES / MAIN

2 whole rainbow trout, about 400 g
   (14 oz) each
100 ml (3½ fl oz) vegetable oil
2 onions, finely sliced
1 teaspoon ground turmeric
1 teaspoon ground cumin
2 teaspoons ground coriander
2 teaspoons red curry powder
1 teaspoon mustard powder
2 cm (¾ inch) piece of ginger, very finely
   chopped
2 garlic cloves, very finely chopped
1 cinnamon stick

2 cloves
6 cardamom pods
750 ml (26 fl oz/3 cups) chicken stock
   or water
50 g (1¾ oz) sultanas
375 g (13 oz/1½ cups) natural Greek
   yoghurt
1 teaspoon cornflour (cornstarch)
2 teaspoons soft brown sugar
12 cherry tomatoes, cut in half
2 tablespoons chopped coriander (cilantro)
   leaves

Wash the rainbow trout inside and out under cold running water, then pat dry with paper towel. Lay the trout on a chopping board and remove and discard the heads (the heads can be cut in half lengthways and cooked in the curry if you like). Working towards the tail, cut the trout into 2 cm (¾ inch) wide cutlets.

Place a large frying pan over high heat, then add one-third of the vegetable oil. When the oil is hot, seal the cutlets for 1 minute on both sides, cooking them in two or three batches. Remove the cutlets from the frying pan, drain on paper towel and set aside.

Wipe the frying pan clean and place it back over medium heat. Add the remaining oil and fry the onions until they start to caramelise, stirring occasionally, for about 15 minutes. During this time, combine the ground spices, curry powder and mustard powder with the ginger and garlic in a bowl. Once the onion has coloured, add the spice mixture to the onions and continue to cook for 5 minutes. Stir in the cinnamon, cloves and cardamom pods and cook for another 2 minutes to combine the flavours. Add the stock a little at a time, and bring it to the boil, then reduce the heat and simmer for 10 minutes.

Meanwhile, put the sultanas in a bowl, cover with hot water and soak for 10 minutes, then drain. Whisk the yoghurt and cornflour together in a bowl. Take the frying pan off the heat and whisk the yoghurt into the curry. Return the pan to the heat, then add the brown sugar, cherry tomatoes and sultanas. Bring the curry to a simmer, add the fish cutlets and cook gently for about 4 minutes, or until the trout is cooked through. Taste and season with salt if required, then garnish with the coriander. Serve with basmati rice.

EATING OUT — DOING YOUR BIT FOR A SUSTAINABLE FUTURE

DOLLAR PER KILOGRAM, SEAFOOD IS THE MOST EXPENSIVE ANIMAL PROTEIN. IT IS THE ONLY FOOD INDUSTRY TO RELY MOSTLY ON WILD STOCK TO MAINTAIN SUPPLY, ALTHOUGH THIS IS CHANGING. THE VAGARIES OF THE WEATHER, FUEL PRICES AND THE NOMADIC NATURE OF THE FISH ALL CONTRIBUTE TO THE PRICE WE PAY FOR OUR SEAFOOD. IT IS SOMETIMES DIFFICULT FOR RESTAURANTS TO LIST SEAFOOD ITEMS ON THEIR MENUS, AS THE BASE COST CAN BE VERY VOLATILE, AFFECTING THE PROFITABILITY OF THE DISH. A SHREWD CHEF WILL BUY SEAFOOD IN SEASON (YES, FISH IS A SEASONAL PRODUCT) AND NEVER SET A PRICE ON THEIR MENU UNLESS THE COST PRICE IS GUARANTEED. THIS IS WHY YOU WILL OFTEN SEE 'FISH OF THE DAY' OR 'MARKET PRICE' LISTED ON MENUS.

The seafood suppliers have a hard job; they have to remain profitable, while balancing what a chef is willing to pay. The type of fish chefs buy and the price they are prepared to pay for it is inexplicably linked to what you are likely to order off a menu and what you are prepared to pay for it. You, the customer, are possibly the most important player in this scenario.

It is the customer who the chefs ultimately have to please. You have to find our menu items appealing otherwise we are out of business. I know from experience what the most popular fish are for a restaurant to sell, those that sell almost in spite of what they are accompanied by. See if the fish on my list corresponds with the fish you last ate or would be inclined to eat in a restaurant: snapper, blue eye, barramundi (wild caught) and tuna. The enormous demand for these species places upward pressure on the price we pay for them and, unfortunately, their popularity is affecting their long-term sustainability. Surprisingly, many chefs don't rank the sustainability of a particular fish species very high on their list of selection criteria — popularity, quality and price seem to be more important. These factors need to be considered if a restaurant is to remain viable. However, if we want to protect the ocean's ecology, the dining public needs to work with the chefs and do their bit for the environment.

Chefs need to be creative with the myriad of lesser-known fish species and you, the customer, need to give them a try; otherwise, we will be locked into a cycle that predicates the use of the few popular ones. I have had a dish of line-caught whole snapper — wok-fried and served with ginger and lime sweet fish sauce — on my menu for the past eight years. During this time I would have literally sold tonnes of it. If you multiply the number of snapper I've sold by the number of restaurants that list snapper on their menus, imagine the total quantity of snapper being consumed daily. This is something that I am very conscious of. I attempt to use lesser-known seafood species, such as leatherjacket, mullet, mulloway and morwong, at Red Lantern, because, for me, they represent more sustainable alternatives. I have had varied success, but I will persevere, as I believe it is the little steps, the things we can do day to day, that will promote and sustain the glorious resource that is seafood.

I LIKE TO USE WESTERN ROCK LOBSTER WHEN IT IS IN SEASON. IT IS ONE OF THE FEW MARINE SPECIES IN AUSTRALIA THAT IS FISHED IN A SUSTAINABLE MANNER.

ROCK LOBSTER SAUTÉED WITH GARLIC, TOMATO & SOFT HERBS

4 SERVES / STARTER

1 x 1.8 kg (4 lb) live rock lobster
2 tablespoons cornflour (cornstarch)
100 ml (3½ fl oz) olive oil
6 garlic cloves, finely sliced
1 onion, finely diced
1 celery stalk, finely diced
2 tablespoons tomato paste
   (concentrated purée)

500 ml (17 fl oz/2 cups) dry rosé wine
2 tomatoes
1 tablespoon chopped oregano
1 tablespoon chopped parsley
1 tablespoon chopped basil

To humanely prepare the lobster, place it in the freezer for 1–2 hours to put it to sleep. Put the lobster on a chopping board and, using a large sharp knife or cleaver, cut through to remove the head. Cut the head in half lengthways, remove the roe and discard it, reserving the head. (The roe can be floured and deep-fried, then used to garnish this dish if you like.) Cut the lobster tail into medallions by cutting through the soft sections of the shell.

Dust the lobster medallions with the cornflour and set aside. Place a large frying pan over medium heat and add half the olive oil. Once the oil is hot, fry the medallions on each side for 1 minute, then remove and set aside.

Wipe the frying pan clean with paper towel, then place the pan back over the heat. Add the remaining oil and fry the lobster head for 2 minutes. Add the garlic, onion and celery and continue to fry until the vegetables are soft but not coloured. Stir through the tomato paste, then gradually add the wine. Bring to the boil, then reduce the heat and simmer for 10 minutes. Remove the lobster head and place it in a bowl. Once cool, pick over the head for pieces of meat, then return the meat to the sauce.

While the lobster is cooking, peel the tomatoes. Score a cross in the base of each tomato. Put the tomatoes in a heatproof bowl and cover with boiling water. Leave for 30–60 seconds, then refresh in a bowl of iced water. Peel the skin away from the cross and discard it, then dice the tomatoes and set aside.

Add the lobster medallions to the pan and cook gently for 3 minutes. Add the tomato and herbs (reserving some for garnish), increase the heat and reduce the sauce quickly until it thickens slightly. Season with sea salt and freshly ground black pepper. Serve garnished with the reserved herbs.

LEATHERJACKET IS VERY UNDERRATED AND IS CONSIDERED A BYCATCH SPECIES, A FISH INADVERTENTLY CAUGHT WHILE PURSUING A MORE VALUABLE PRIZE. I THINK IT HAS AN AMAZING TEXTURE, IT CAN CARRY BIG FLAVOURS SUCH AS LEMONGRASS, SOY OR CURRY SPICES, AND, ONCE COOKED, THE FLESH JUST SLIDES OFF THE BONE.

LEATHERJACKET OVEN-ROASTED WITH LEMONGRASS & GARLIC

4 SERVES / MAIN

4 lemongrass stems
8 garlic cloves, finely chopped
2 bird's eye chillies, finely chopped
2½ tablespoons fish sauce
2 tablespoons sugar
juice of 1 lemon
4 x 350 g (12 oz) leatherjackets (these are usually sold with the heads and skin removed)

2 lemons, halved
1 handful of coriander (cilantro) sprigs

SPRING ONION OIL
3 tablespoons vegetable oil
3 spring onions (scallions), green part only, finely sliced

To make the spring onion oil, place the vegetable oil and spring onion greens in a small saucepan over medium heat. Cook the spring onions until they just start to simmer in the oil, then remove the pan from the heat. Allow the spring onions to cool in the oil.

Peel the tough outer leaves off the lemongrass. Finely slice the bottom white 6–8 cm (2½–3¼ inch) section, then chop very finely. To make the marinade, combine the chopped lemongrass, garlic, chilli, fish sauce, sugar, lemon juice and spring onion oil in a bowl, stirring until the sugar dissolves.

Lay the fish on a chopping board and make four diagonal cuts along the flesh, not quite through to the bone. Repeat the process on the other side. Once you have prepared all of the leatherjackets, place them in a large non-reactive dish. Rub the marinade evenly into all the fish and place in the fridge to marinate for 1 hour.

Preheat the oven to 180°C (350°F/Gas 4). Remove the fish from the fridge and allow it to come back to room temperature. Place the fish on a baking tray with the lemon halves and cook for 20 minutes, or until the flesh is opaque to the bone. Serve garnished with the coriander sprigs.

ONE OF MY FIRST JOBS AS AN APPRENTICE CHEF WAS TO PREPARE AND COOK FISH AND CHIPS. AT THE TIME WE USED FLATHEAD, MAINLY BECAUSE IT WAS FASHIONABLE, AND I WOULD FILLET TEN KILOGRAMS OF IT A DAY TO KEEP UP WITH DEMAND. I'M USING FLATHEAD HERE JUST AS I DID EIGHTEEN YEARS AGO, ALTHOUGH FOR A COMPLETELY DIFFERENT REASON — FLATHEAD IS A SHALLOW WATER FISH AND IS CONSIDERED A VERY SUSTAINABLE SPECIES.

FISH & POTATO SCALLOPS

4 SERVES / MAIN

500 g (1 lb 2 oz) older potatoes, such as
    king edward, spunta or sebago
600 g (1 lb 5 oz) skinless flathead fillets
150 g (5½ oz/1 cup) self-raising flour, plus
    50 g (1¾ oz/⅓ cup) extra
1 teaspoon salt

1 teaspoon baking powder
330 ml (11¼ fl oz) beer (1 small bottle)
vegetable oil, for deep-frying
2 lemons, halved
100 g (3½ oz) garlic mayonnaise
    (page 69)

Wash but do not peel the potatoes, then place them in a saucepan. Cover with cold water, bring to the boil and cook the potatoes until you can pass a skewer through the middle of one; you should feel the tiniest bit of resistance. Drain and set aside to cool. When they are cool enough to handle, peel the skin. Place the potatoes on a tray in the fridge for 30 minutes. Cut the flathead fillets into 10 cm (4 inch) long pieces. Refrigerate until you are ready to cook.

Meanwhile, place the flour in a bowl with the salt and baking powder. Gradually mix the beer through the flour with a fork, being careful not to overmix — a few lumps are OK. Refrigerate the batter.

Preheat the oven to 180°C (350°F/Gas 4). Remove the potatoes from the fridge and cut them lengthways into 1 cm (½ inch) wide pieces. Heat the oil in a large heavy-based frying pan or deep-fryer to 180°C (350°F), or until a cube of bread dropped into the oil turns golden brown in 15 seconds.

While the oil is heating, place the extra flour in a shallow bowl. Dredge the fish pieces and potatoes through the flour and set aside. Remove the batter from the fridge and pass the potato scallops through the batter, gently shaking off any excess. Carefully add the potato scallops to the hot oil, frying a few pieces at a time to maintain the oil temperature, and cook until golden brown. Remove and drain on paper towel, then put in the oven to keep warm. Clean the oil with a wire strainer as you go, then deep-fry the fish in a similar manner. Season with sea salt and serve with the lemon halves and garlic mayonnaise.

CONTENTS

OULTRY 127

POULTRY

IT'S ALMOST IMPOSSIBLE TO IMAGINE, BUT NOT SO LONG AGO
IT WAS CONSIDERED A LUXURY TO HAVE A ROAST CHICKEN
ON THE SUBURBAN DINNER TABLE. WHEN MY FATHER WAS A
TEENAGER, A ROAST CHICKEN WAS A CELEBRATORY DISH TO BE
SAVOURED ON SPECIAL OCCASIONS. IT WAS CUSTOMARY THEN
FOR MY GRANDFATHER TO BRING SIX CHICKS HOME IN LATE
SEPTEMBER. THEIR ARRIVAL CAUSED MUCH EXCITEMENT; THIS
MEANT CHRISTMAS WAS ONLY THREE MONTHS AWAY. IT TAKES
A CHICKEN, ON A NATURAL GRAIN DIET SUPPLEMENTED WITH THE
ODD FORAGED WORM AND INSECT, THREE MONTHS TO REACH A
SIZE WHERE IT IS SUITABLE FOR THE DINING TABLE. THE PRIZED
CHICKENS WERE FREE TO ROAM IN THE BACKYARD BY DAY AND
HOUSED IN A COOP AT NIGHT. MY GRANDMOTHER WOULD KEEP
A WATCHFUL EYE OVER 'CHRISTMAS DINNER' AS SHE SET ABOUT
HER DAILY DUTIES. THIS CUSTOM STARTED LONG BEFORE I
WAS BORN AND THE RELEVANCE OF IT WAS INITIALLY LOST ON
ME. I BELONG TO A GENERATION THAT HAS ALWAYS KNOWN
COMMERCIALLY PROCESSED CHICKEN.

Prior to the 1960s, if you wanted a chicken for dinner more often than not you had to
rear it yourself. The commercial chicken meat industry began in the late fifties when new
strains of chicken were developed for the sole purpose of producing meat. It is estimated
that the industry began with 3 million chickens; today the Australian chicken industry
produces approximately 460 million birds annually. About 4 per cent of these chickens
are raised by free-range farming, and half again are reared organically.

Intensively farmed chickens dominate the marketplace and offer an inexpensive animal-
based protein alternative to beef, lamb and pork, but at what cost to the animals themselves?
Intuitively, most people would say buying free-range and organically raised chicken is both
ethically and environmentally more responsible. As an urban cook this notion comes
naturally — I like to imagine the animal I am about to prepare or serve has lived an ideal life,
roaming freely about the farm, pecking at the ground, eating insects and grass seed. But do
chickens really live better lives on free-range and organic farms? And more importantly, is it
ethically more responsible of us to buy free-range and organic chicken?

Let's first look at some of the factors that influence our decision to buy either
intensively farmed, free-range or organically raised chicken.

PRICE

I once conducted a survey whereby I simply stood on the footpath outside my restaurant
and asked about fifty people passing by if they buy whole chicken from the supermarket
and, if so, what factors influence their decision to buy one type of chicken over another.
Overwhelmingly the majority of people said their decision was based on price, and that
they tended to buy the cheaper one.

Intensively farmed chicken is the cheapest at the cash register given the total integration of production and its economy of scale. Free-range chicken is next, with higher production costs and lower housing density. Organically raised chickens are the most expensive to produce, as strict environmental and ethical regulations control all aspects of their production.

ETHICS

There is a growing appreciation for free-range chicken, although I'm not entirely convinced that everyone who buys free-range does so for its superior flavour. Many buy free-range because they believe it is the ethically responsible thing to do. That may be, but this decision is sometimes made because of the misconception that intensively farmed chickens are raised in cages, which is totally incorrect. However, I do applaud consumers who stop and think about the consequences of their purchases and encourage more people to do so.

TASTE

At Red Lantern we serve chicken that is pasture-raised and fed a mixture of grains and cereals especially blended on the farm. Our chickens range freely, live a stress-free life and are protected from predators by Maremma sheepdogs. Importantly, the chickens are processed on the farm, eliminating undue stress caused by transporting them to the slaughterhouse. They are collected at night when they are more settled and processed early the next morning. I feel you can taste the tranquillity of the chicken in the meat and the firm texture of the flesh, which only develops when the chickens have had the freedom to run around, dust-bath and flap their wings.

According to my own survey, a lot of people buy intensively farmed chicken because it is cheaper, but I wonder if these people have ever tasted free-range or organically grown chicken to appreciate the difference in taste and texture?

Choice magazine in Australia conducted a taste test, comparing the flavour of chickens reared by the three different farming methods: intensive, free-range and organic. All the chickens weighed the same, and were simply roasted without using salt and pepper — roasted in the buff so to speak. The judging panel were given a slice of breast and a slice of leg meat and asked to critique the flavour and texture of the meat. I had assumed they would proclaim an obvious difference in the flavour of the chickens. To my surprise, the judges concluded that no chicken stood out from another, and all agreed none of them tasted much like the roast chicken they ate when they were children. I have trouble accepting these results, and I'm sure I'm not the only one. I feel there is an obvious difference in the flavour and, just as importantly, the texture of the differently raised chickens. Food and flavour is inextricably bound to time and place — it is possible for memory and the perception of a flavour or meal to be embellished by the passing of time. Could this explain the judges' recollection of the taste of the chicken from their childhood?

If there really is no discernible difference in the flavour of the chickens, then perhaps a convincing argument could be presented for buying the least expensive one? But are the environmental and ethical costs of production fully represented in the price we pay at the cash register? In the case of the intensively raised chicken, it is the chicken that pays the ultimate price.

INTENSIVE CHICKEN FARMING

The intensive farming of meat chickens, also known as broilers, really took flight in Australia in the 1970s. During this decade there was a rapid increase in consumer demand for chicken meat, which can, in part, be attributed to a certain white-haired, bearded and moustached gentleman from Kentucky, named Colonel Harland Sanders.

In 1968 Canadian-born Bob Lapointe opened the first Kentucky Fried Chicken store in Guildford in western Sydney. During the 1970s, as more than seventy-five KFC stores opened across the country, chicken production increased by 38 per cent. By the end of the decade this figure more than doubled as the Australian appetite for chicken products grew exponentially and new technologies were adopted by the industry to satisfy demand.

Three companies produce the majority of all intensively farmed chicken in Australia — Bartter Enterprises, Ingham Enterprises and Baiada. All are family owned and have grown over the decades from small farms to large vertically integrated companies with their own breeding, feed producing, growing, processing and packaging facilities. This total control of the production process has many economic benefits for the companies, and for consumers this means an uninterrupted supply of affordable chicken. But are the chickens getting a fair deal?

THE LACK OF GENETIC DIVERSITY

During the 1970s, breakthroughs in genetic science meant breeders were able to identify the specific traits they believed would make a chicken better suited to the intensive farm environment. The industry desired a chicken that would efficiently convert the food it ate into muscle mass, had strong bones and a docile temperament. Over time, chickens were selectively bred until the industry managed to produce a bird that fulfilled these requirements. Although there are literally hundreds of different chicken breeds, the modern broiler's ancestry is apparently linked to just three.

Breeding companies compete with each other to develop and sell the superior broiler. Naturally, these companies keep the genetic make-up of their chickens a secret, which is why it is now so difficult to pinpoint the exact breed of a broiler chicken. It wasn't always this complicated, as the name of a chicken breed was once synonymous with the country or territory from which it came. Today broilers tend to be named after the companies that created them and have names better suited to industrial machines than chickens, such as the unappetisingly named Cobb 500.

Some scientists believe it is dangerous for the poultry industry to rely on the genes of just three chicken breeds. This lack of genetic diversity could leave them vulnerable to new diseases; or defective genetic material in just one chicken could have devastating consequences further down the line.

THE GROWTH RATE OF THE CHICKENS

Contrary to popular belief, hormones have not played a role in the accelerated growth rates of the modern-day chicken (however, they were once used as an alternative to castration to improve eating quality). Instead, this has been achieved through selective breeding and improvements in diet. Chicken feed is nutritionally tailored to suit every stage of the chickens' development. Breeding stock is fed a low-protein diet supplemented with calcium and minerals for healthy fetal development and strong eggshells, whereas the chickens destined for the dinner table are fed a high-protein diet to build muscle mass quickly. Chickens now reach a marketable weight within a staggering 5 to 7 weeks. This rapid growth, with lower food consumption, is incredible, but it does come at a cost to the well-being of the birds. The rapid growth rate places stress on the chicken's skeletal system and many suffer from leg malformation and heart failure.

ANTIBIOTICS

The intensive chicken industry does use antibiotics but guidelines exist for their use. Antibiotics are used to prevent serious diseases occurring or to treat chickens in the case of a bacterial outbreak, and can only be administered by a veterinarian, using only those antibiotics not used to treat human ailments. After the antibiotics have been given, there must be a withholding period before processing to ensure there is no antibiotic residue in the meat. Unlike the practice in other countries, the antibiotics used by the chicken industry in Australia do not promote growth.

THE ARTIFICIAL ENVIRONMENT IN THE SHEDS

Every aspect of the environment within a poultry shed is controlled and manipulated to ensure chickens grow quickly and efficiently. Broilers are housed in sheds of varying sizes, but typically a modern shed is approximately 150 metres long by 15 metres wide. Sophisticated electronically controlled ventilation systems are used to maintain a constant temperature within a modern poultry shed. Chicks spend the first few days of their life contained in a special brooding area where the temperature is kept at approximately 30 degrees Celsius. From here, farmers can easily monitor the chicks' progress, and the warm temperature helps limit juvenile mortality. As the chicks grow the temperature is lowered and maintained between 21 and 23 degrees Celsius. This range represents the optimum temperature for food conversion and enhanced growth. If the temperature is too low, the chickens will eat more but use energy from the food to keep their bodies warm. If it is too high, they eat less and don't gain weight effectively. Keeping the lights dim in the sheds for up to 20 hours a day also encourages the birds to eat more and gain weight quickly.

OVERCROWDING IN SHEDS

Approximately 40 000 to 60 000 chickens are housed in a poultry shed at any one time. Stocking densities are set by government policy and vary between 28 kilograms and 40 kilograms per square metre, depending on the shed design and the time of year. Initially, when the chickens are released into the sheds there is plenty of room to move around and explore. However, as the chickens grow, 'personal' space becomes a serious issue. When chickens reach specific sizes and weights throughout the 5 to 7 week growing cycle they are periodically harvested to fulfil market requirements. Although this reduces the number of chickens in the shed, the chickens still struggle to move freely. By the end of their lives, the chickens will only have a 25 centimetre square area of the shed floor to claim as their own.

Chickens on intensive farms are food-converting machines and their growth is not left to chance. Every aspect of their environment is artificially controlled to ensure the 'machine' doesn't stop working before harvest time.

CLEANLINESS OF THE SHEDS

Poultry shed floors are made of concrete or compressed clay, which are covered with litter made from rice hulls or sawdust. The litter provides bedding and loose organic material in which the chickens can exercise their natural foraging and scratching tendencies. The humidity in the shed is closely monitored. If it is too high, the litter can become damp or wet; if it's too low, the dry conditions will create dust particles that can affect the chickens' respiratory systems and eyes.

Maintaining clean litter should be a priority for the industry, but unfortunately the litter is seldom changed during the growing cycle, so the chickens spend most of their lives foraging and scratching in litter covered with their own excrement. Chicken faeces contains harmful bacteria that promote the spread of disease, and the high levels of ammonia present can burn the skin of the chickens' legs and feet.

At best, the floors are cleaned when the chickens are moved for processing, but ideally the growing sheds need to be thoroughly cleaned with high-pressure hoses and antiseptic. They should be left empty for up to 2 weeks, depending on the size of the operation, before restocking to reduce the chance of pathogens from the previous stock infecting the new stock.

TRANSPORTING CHICKENS TO THE SLAUGHTERHOUSES

Chickens suffer undue stress in intensive farming systems and it is a major ethical concern. To this end, government codes of practice stipulate the correct procedure for the transporting and slaughtering of poultry, and outline the minimum standard of care and responsibility of the poultry producers, although many people believe these codes don't offer adequate protection. When the chickens are ready to be processed they are transported by truck to the abattoir, usually located within a 100-kilometre radius of the growing sheds. During transportation, it is the responsibility of the owners of the poultry operation to ensure the well-being of the chickens. The poultry industry is predominantly self-regulated and I am confident most farmers follow the right procedures, but who is ultimately responsible for ensuring these codes of practice are upheld? To make things more complicated, animal welfare standards vary from state to state within Australia. This lack of uniformity only adds to consumer confusion.

Intensive chicken farming deserves the criticism it attracts. The chickens within the system are treated more like machines than living creatures, although I'm sure the industry would disagree with me. Even though codes of practice exist, I don't feel they offer the necessary protection. The chickens pay the ultimate price for the few dollars saved at the cash register; those savings certainly aren't enough to validate the industry. Science has played a key role in the 'success' of the intensive chicken industry, from the rearing of the chicks through to the treatment of the waste the industry generates. Theoretically, the industry has the expertise and resources to address all of the issues I have raised. Until consumers are completely confident that animal welfare standards are improved and upheld and bad practitioners are fined or banned from operating, I believe the industry will continue to have its critics.

FREE-RANGE CHICKEN PRODUCTION

Free-range chickens offer a better alternative to intensively raised chickens primarily because of the better standards of general welfare. Chickens on a free-range farm are raised in a similar fashion to those on an intensive farm but there are some distinct differences. Interestingly, many intensive farms also raise free-range chickens.

As the name suggests, free-range chickens are required to have access to open pasture during daylight hours and are housed in sheds at night to protect them from predators. The chickens can roam outdoors, stretch their wings and exercise. Inside, there is more room to move around because the sheds are stocked at a lower density, approximately 28 kilograms or less per square metre.

But the free-range industry also has its critics. We have no way of knowing whether the chickens actually do venture outside. Food and water is constantly available inside the sheds and critics claim the chickens therefore have little incentive to range outside. The industry is predominately self-regulated so the onus is really on the individual producer to do the right thing. I believe the majority of farmers do follow best farm practice, but how can we be sure? An industry insider once told me the only time an inspector steps on his property is when he mandatorily reports an outbreak of disease. Perhaps if the industry was independently inspected, we, as consumers, would have more faith in the system.

Free-range chickens, like those that are intensively raised, are not given growth-promoting hormones. And similar rules apply for the use of antibiotics, except for one major difference. When free-range chickens are given antibiotics they can no longer be sold as 'free-range' (these are then usually sold as intensively produced chickens). This is why some operators raise chickens using both production methods — no chickens are wasted in the process.

The genetic stock of both free-range and intensive chickens is, for the most part, identical. Farmers of free-range chickens tend to buy their day-old chicks from one of the three main breeding companies. The chicks have the genetic disposition for accelerated growth. These birds are born hungry, and they grow at a similar rate in a free-range environment as they do in an intensive system. I was surprised to learn the free-range chickens I use in my restaurant are processed at 5 to 7 weeks, the same age as for intensively raised chickens. I had always assumed the flavour of free-range chickens was enhanced because, among other factors, they lived longer. But perhaps it is the freedom free-range chickens have to move around and exercise, all the while building muscle mass, that gives them more flavour.

If similarities can be drawn between intensively raised and free-range chickens, then, equally, similarities can be drawn between free-range and organic chickens.

ORGANICALLY RAISED CHICKEN

Why have I used the term 'organically raised' chicken? Why not 'organic chicken'? This is because producers of organic chicken still have to buy the majority of their stock as day-old chicks from the commercial breeding companies. To date, I know of just one organic producer with a breeding facility large enough to produce the number of chicks necessary to satisfy demand. This has the potential to change of course, given time.

Similarities exist in the production methods of free-range and organically raised chickens, so what are they, and what are the differences?

IT TAKES A DAY-OLD CHICK ONLY 5 TO 7 WEEKS TO REACH A MARKETABLE WEIGHT OF 1.8 KILOGRAMS. THIS HAS BEEN ACHIEVED THROUGH SELECTIVE BREEDING AND HIGH-PROTEIN FEED, AND NOT, AS IS COMMONLY THOUGHT, DUE TO GROWTH HORMONES.

The term 'organic' in the farming context relates to the way in which food is produced. Typically this is characterised by a more holistic approach to production, free of artificial pesticides and fertilisers. Like the free-range industry, the use of antibiotics is strictly forbidden during organic chicken production. Natural remedies are used to treat disease but, for the most part, it's the individual farmer's skill to best manage his flock that offers the most protection from disease.

For organic chickens this means better standards of practice are certified to ensure better living conditions and to maintain the environmental health of the production system. It is the most expensive form of production because it is very labour intensive. The maintenance of the farm ecology is crucial, as any lapse in the rudimentary standard of production could affect the health of the chickens.

'Biodynamic' is seen as the pinnacle of organic farm practice. This involves the farm operating as a self-contained or closed-cycle ecosystem whereby all aspects of production occur on the farm. In simple terms, this means grain for chicken food is grown on the farm, the chickens eat the grains, range and forage freely on the farm, and any waste they produce is composted and used as fertiliser to maintain soil health. This cycle continuously repeats itself.

Regardless of how chickens are raised, the composition of the food they eat is essentially the same. What distinguishes the organic industry from the others is that the food fed to the chickens must be sourced and certified from organic farms. Worldwide less grain is grown organically, therefore grain prices are very volatile. Farmers compete with other industries that use organic grain and consequently it can cost up to twice as much as ordinary grain. Ironically, the organic chickens themselves are a 'problem' in that they live for up to twice as long as their commercial counterparts and therefore eat twice as much grain. To help reduce costs and to ensure supply, some of the larger producers grow their own organic grains.

Organic chickens are also kept in sheds at night for protection against predators and harsh weather conditions. The sheds have a typical stocking density of 25 kilograms per square metre, similar to the stocking levels of the free-range industry. Organic chickens are required to have access to the range areas adjacent to the barns from 10 days old (free-range chicks have access to pasture after 21 days). This extra time exercising and foraging on grass and insects, combined with the fact that they are not processed until they are 65 to 80 days old, improves the texture and flavour of the meat.

The same rules and regulations apply for the transport and slaughter of organic chicken as for the other methods of production. Organic abattoirs do exist, however some organic growers have accredited slaughtering facilities on site.

Perhaps the best thing from a consumer's point of view is that organic farms have the most stringent rules and regulations governing production. Farm accreditation is provided by organisations approved by the Australian Quarantine Inspection Service, and the organic farms are subject to independent inspections (unlike free-range farms, which have their own inspectors).

Organic chickens may reap the benefits of 'best practice' farm procedures, but I'm not so sure the farmers do. I once used organic chickens in my restaurant. I found the birds to be of superior flavour, but the price and reliability of supply was a concern. I bought from a small producer who was exceptionally passionate about the chickens in his care.

But often his birds would be of different sizes and their price would fluctuate to cover production expenses. I appreciate an organic farmer's job is a difficult one. Rain and floods may mean the farmers are flooded in and can't transport their chicken to market, and high organic grain prices could restrict their ability to buy food — all of this affects the farm's profitability.

The organic farming industry is an admirable one, one that marries farming traditions of the past with the science of the future. I can appreciate why chickens raised by this method are the most expensive given the higher production costs, but do they represent value for money? The answer to this depends on your perception of the organic industry in general. I believe free-range and organic chickens taste better. When you buy organic chickens you are supporting the organic food chain and the organic producers who nurture the environment. Ethically, from the animal husbandry point of view, free-range chickens have similar living conditions to organic chickens with access to foraging ranges and limited shed stocking densities. It is also worth noting that there are free-range farmers — like the farmer who raises the chickens I use in my restaurant — who raise chickens to organic standards but can't sell their birds as organic because, for one reason or another, they don't seek organic certification.

THE NEED FOR BETTER LABELLING

I have a personal preference for free-range and organically raised chicken. I cannot support the intensive poultry industry as it exists today. If animal welfare standards were dramatically improved, then perhaps, ethically speaking, there might be a place for the industry in the future. Theoretically, it is possible to create a near perfect environment to raise chickens. I, like the majority of you, believe that environment already exists — free-range and organic.

Unfortunately, 96 per cent of all the chickens produced in Australia are produced intensively. Regrettably, it appears the intensive poultry industry is here to stay. But how can we ever have confidence in an industry that was essentially created to put cheap meat on the table — cheap meat produced with almost total disregard for animal welfare.

I feel the answer lies with the regulatory body that governs the industry. We, the consumers, need to feel confident that a single entity will ensure the best for the animals' welfare and, most importantly, enforce the law. At present there is no way of distinguishing the farmers who are operating to the best farm practice from those who are not. We have no way of identifying which producers are, for example, stocking their sheds with fewer chickens and cleaning the chicken litter throughout the growing process. If these issues were identified, then perhaps (and it's a huge 'perhaps') I would consider buying a chicken raised exclusively in a poultry shed.

The most important factor in this whole debate is the need for a national labelling system. Details of the production method and, more importantly, the standard of husbandry used during production need to be clearly and easily identifiable by the consumer. If this system existed, we could reward the companies using better standards of husbandry by purchasing their chickens. Potentially this would create a system where competition for our shopping dollars was waged on ethical grounds.

WE NEED TO UNDERSTAND HOW CHICKENS ARE RAISED IN THE DIFFERENT PRODUCTION SYSTEMS SO WE CAN MAKE INFORMED PURCHASING DECISIONS. WE CAST A VOTE IN SUPPORT FOR ONE SYSTEM OR ANOTHER EVERY TIME WE BUY A CHICKEN. WHENEVER WE BUY ETHICALLY AND SUSTAINABLY PRODUCED CHICKEN WE ARE TELLING RETAILERS AND FARMERS WE CARE AND RESPECT HOW THESE CHICKENS ARE RAISED. INDUSTRY IS DRIVEN BY THE BOTTOM LINE AND, OVER TIME, INDUSTRY DOES RESPOND TO THE CHOICES WE MAKE AT THE CHECKOUT.

VIETNAMESE CHICKEN NOODLE SOUP

6 SERVES / MAIN

1 kg (2 lb 4 oz) fresh thin rice noodles
   (banh pho)
1 white onion, cut into fine rings
3 spring onions (scallions), finely sliced
250 g (9 oz) bean sprouts
½ bunch of Thai basil, picked
½ bunch of coriander (cilantro), picked
2 limes, each cut into 3 wedges
3 bird's eye chillies, finely sliced
4 tablespoons fish sauce

SOUP BASE
1 x 1.8 kg (4 lb) chicken
1 large onion, skin on, cut in half
½ garlic bulb, sliced horizontally
3 cm (1¼ inch) piece of ginger, cut in half
   lengthways
2 star anise
1 cinnamon stick
2 cloves
3 tablespoons fish sauce
1 tablespoon caster (superfine) sugar

To make the soup base, first wash the chicken inside and out under cold running water. Fit it snugly into a stockpot and cover with 4 litres (140 fl oz/16 cups) of water. Chargrill the onion, garlic and ginger until slightly blackened. Scrape off any pieces that are really burnt, then place the onion, garlic and ginger in the pot, along with the spices, fish sauce and sugar. Place the pot over high heat and bring to the boil, then reduce the heat and simmer gently for 1 hour.

   Remove the chicken from the stock and place it on a plate to cool. Once the chicken has cooled, remove the skin and shred the meat into small pieces. Pass the stock through a fine sieve into another saucepan.

   Have a saucepan of water boiling on the stovetop. Blanch the rice noodles, in three batches, in the boiling water. Divide each batch of noodles between two serving bowls. Distribute the shredded chicken, onion rings, spring onion, bean sprouts, Thai basil and coriander on top of the noodles. Bring the reserved stock to a rapid boil, then ladle it into the bowls. Serve the soup with the lime wedges, chilli and fish sauce on the side.

BACK TO EDEN
"A" 30 SYDNEY MKTS

THE URBAN COOK | POULTRY

CHICKEN BRAISED WITH WHITE WINE, CREAM & THYME

4 SERVES / MAIN

- 4 large chicken marylands (chicken leg quarters), cage bone attached, trimmed of excess fat and skin
- 2 tablespoons olive oil
- 2 carrots, cut into 4 cm (1½ inch) lengths, then quartered
- 8 French shallots or very small new season onions
- ½ small bunch of thyme or lemon thyme
- 2 garlic cloves, peeled, crushed with the side of a knife
- 250 ml (9 fl oz/1 cup) white wine, such as riesling
- 125 ml (4 fl oz/½ cup) pouring cream (35% fat)
- ½ teaspoon sea salt
- ½ teaspoon freshly ground black pepper
- pinch of cayenne pepper
- 2 teaspoons plain (all-purpose) flour
- 10 g (¼ oz) butter

Wash the chicken, then dry with paper towel. Place a large deep frying pan (about 30 cm/ 12 inches wide) over medium heat. Add the olive oil and fry the chicken, skin side down, for 3–4 minutes until the skin is golden brown. Turn and continue to fry for 2 minutes, then remove the chicken from the pan and drain on paper towel.

Carefully pour off any excess fat and wipe the frying pan clean with paper towel, then return the chicken to the pan with the carrots, shallots, thyme, garlic and wine. Place over high heat and bring the wine to the boil, then reduce the heat to low, cover with a lid and braise for 30 minutes. If you do not have a large frying pan, you can put the chicken in a roasting tin, cover it with foil and braise on the stovetop or in a 180°C (350°F/Gas 4) oven.

After 30 minutes, remove the lid and add the cream, then season with the sea salt, black pepper and cayenne pepper. Continue to cook for 15–20 minutes, or until the chicken is succulent and almost falling from the bone. Remove the chicken and vegetables with a slotted spoon to a dish and keep warm. Bring the sauce up to a simmer.

Combine the flour and butter in a small bowl to form a paste, then whisk into the simmering sauce. Simmer for a couple of minutes to cook out the flour and thicken the sauce. Taste and adjust the seasoning if necessary, then serve the sauce over the chicken.

SIMPLE YELLOW CURRY OF CHICKEN, BASIL & BAMBOO SHOOTS

4-6 SERVES / MAIN

3 tablespoons vegetable oil
1.2 kg (2 lb 10 oz) mixed chicken drumsticks, thighs and wings, or use 800 g (1 lb 12 oz) boneless, skinless chicken thighs
800 ml (28 fl oz) coconut cream
2 tablespoons Malaysian curry powder
1 tablespoon ground turmeric
100 g (3½ oz) shredded bamboo shoots, washed under cold water
4 kaffir lime (makrut) leaves, finely sliced
1 tablespoon finely grated ginger
2 tablespoons finely chopped lemongrass, white part only
1 tablespoon finely chopped garlic
2 tablespoons finely chopped red Asian shallots or onion
4 tablespoons fish sauce
50 g (¾ oz) palm sugar (jaggery), grated
1 teaspoon salt
1 large handful of Thai basil leaves

Heat the oil in a wok or large frying pan, add the chicken pieces and seal on all sides until golden, then remove the chicken from the wok and drain on paper towel. If using boneless chicken thighs, you can ignore this step.

Wipe the wok clean and place it over medium–high heat. Add 100 ml (3½ fl oz) of the coconut cream, bring it to the boil and continue to boil rapidly for 2 minutes. Add the curry powder, turmeric, bamboo shoots and chicken pieces (or if using the chicken thighs, add them now). Stir well to combine the flavours.

Add the lime leaves, ginger, lemongrass, garlic and shallots. Stir well, then add the remaining coconut cream. Bring the cream to the boil, then reduce the heat and simmer for 20–30 minutes. When the chicken is cooked through and tender, increase the heat and season the curry with the fish sauce, palm sugar and salt. Stir through the Thai basil and serve with jasmine rice.

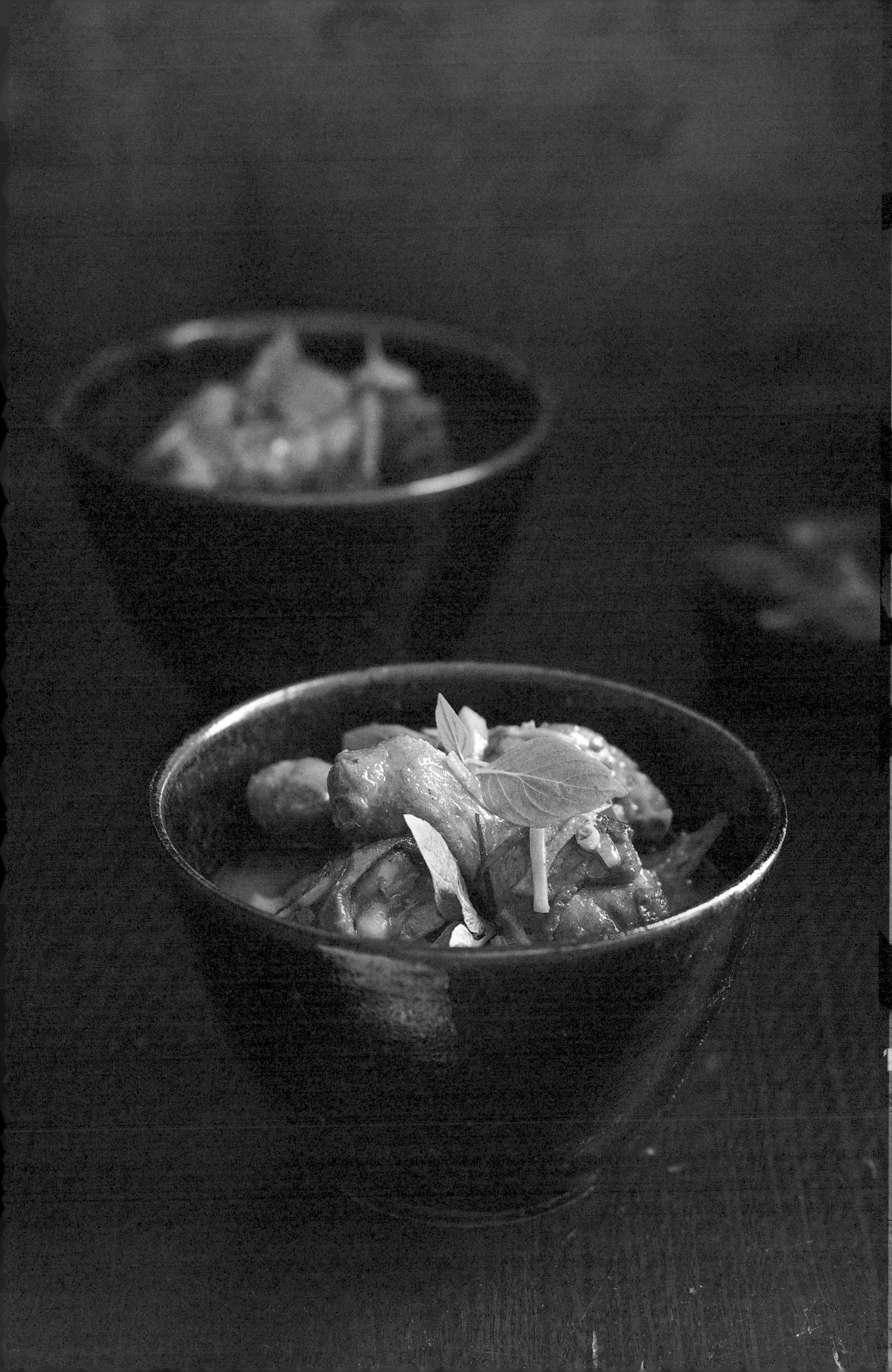

I HAD TO INCLUDE MY MUM'S RECIPE FOR ROAST CHICKEN IN THIS BOOK. HER STRAIGHTFORWARD APPROACH TO GOOD HOUSEKEEPING AND SEASONAL COOKING SUSTAINED AND NOURISHED OUR FAMILY. MUM TAUGHT ME THAT IT IS POSSIBLE TO MAKE DELICIOUS FOOD WITH JUST THREE OR FOUR KEY INGREDIENTS, BECAUSE A GREAT RECIPE DOES NOT NECESSARILY HAVE TO BE A COMPLICATED ONE.

MY MUM'S ROAST CHICKEN

4 SERVES / MAIN

1 x 1.8 kg (4 lb) chicken
1 small garlic bulb, cut in half horizontally
½ lemon
1 teaspoon olive oil

2 teaspoons sea salt
1 teaspoon freshly ground black pepper
2 carrots
3–4 tablespoons chicken stock or water

Preheat the oven to 200°C (400°F/Gas 6). Wash the chicken inside and out under cold running water, then pat dry with paper towel. Rub the garlic and lemon all over the skin, then place both inside the chicken. Now rub the skin with the olive oil and season well with the sea salt and black pepper. I like to seal the chicken cavity by placing kitchen string under the bottom of the carcass, then drawing it up to form a figure of eight around the legs. Tie it off to secure.

Cut the carrots into 2 cm (¾ inch) thick disks and place them in a roasting tin. Place the chicken on top of the carrot, with the chicken breast facing up. Roast for 20 minutes, then carefully remove the tin from the oven. Turn the chicken on its side and reduce the oven to 180°C (350°F/Gas 4). Return the chicken to the oven and roast for another 15 minutes. Turn the chicken over to the remaining side and roast for a further 15 minutes, then remove it from the oven. To test if the chicken is done, pierce the thickest part of the leg with a skewer — the juices will run clear. Loosely cover the chicken with foil and allow to rest for 10 minutes.

While the chicken is resting, make a simple sauce from the juices in the roasting tin. Pour the juices into a small saucepan and skim off the fat. Place the saucepan over high heat, add the chicken stock or water and bring to the boil. Season with sea salt and freshly ground black pepper and serve over the carved chicken.

THE CHICKEN BEFORE THE EGG

I ALWAYS USE FREE-RANGE, ORGANIC OR BIODYNAMIC EGGS IN MY COOKING. ALTHOUGH THE PHILOSOPHIES BEHIND THESE FARMING METHODS ARE QUITE DIFFERENT, AT THEIR CORE THEY ALL VALUE HAPPY, HEALTHY CHICKENS. THE CHICKENS RAISED ON THESE FARMS CAN MOVE FREELY AND ACT OUT NATURAL TENDENCIES. CHICKENS NEED ROOM TO MOVE, STRETCH THEIR WINGS AND FORAGE, AND THOSE CONFINED IN CLOSE QUARTERS SUFFER ADVERSELY.

When stressed, chickens engage in compulsive behaviour and act out aggressively by pecking at each other. A chicken's beak is extremely sensitive, they use it to perceive and explore the world around them. It is also used as a tool to work out the hierarchy within the flock, commonly known as the pecking order. In a caged egg production system, the young chicks have the tip of their beaks seared off (the beaks of broiler chickens are not routinely trimmed, as they tend to be more docile in nature). The chickens are still able to eat and drink, but they are less likely to injure or kill each other when acting out in frustration. Needless to say, this practice is not viewed favourably outside the industry and serious welfare concerns surround most facets of caged egg production.

In this modern age, I see no reason for this barbaric and archaic industry to exist. It exists for what? To save you, on average, less than 10 cents per egg. The next time you shop for eggs, I recommend, at the very least, you consider buying free-range.

SPIEDINI OF CHICKEN LIVER, SPECK & BLACK OLIVE

4 SERVES / STARTER

8 strong rosemary sprigs
500 g (1 lb 2 oz) chicken livers, cleaned
   of sinew and cut into 16 pieces
250 g (9 oz) speck, cut into 16 pieces,
   or use thick bacon pieces

16 black olives, pitted
16 sage leaves
2 tablespoons olive oil

Remove the leaves from the rosemary sprigs, leaving a thatch of leaves on the top of each sprig. Sharpen the denuded end into a point. Thread a piece of chicken liver onto the rosemary spear followed by a piece of speck, an olive and a doubled-over sage leaf, then repeat. Repeat the process until you have assembled eight spiedini. Place them on a serving plate, drizzle with the olive oil and season with sea salt and freshly ground black pepper.

Heat a chargrill pan or frying pan over medium heat. Place the well-oiled spiedini in the pan and cook for about 2 minutes each side; the livers should be well seared on the outside and pink in the middle. Remove from the pan and allow to rest in a warm place for 2 minutes before serving. Serve with a green salad.

IT'S IMPORTANT TO TRY TO USE ALL PARTS OF THE CHICKEN. THIS IS A QUICK AND EASY WAY TO ENJOY CHICKEN LIVERS. IF YOU PREFER, YOU CAN SUBSTITUTE THE SPECK OR BACON WITH MUSHROOMS.

154

YOU CAN EITHER COOK A WHOLE CHICKEN FOR THIS SALAD, FOLLOWING THE RECIPE FOR THE VIETNAMESE CHICKEN NOODLE SOUP (PAGE 142), OR USE LEFTOVER ROAST CHICKEN. BANANA BLOSSOM OXIDISES AND DISCOLOURS QUICKLY, SO PREPARE IT JUST BEFORE YOU NEED IT, THEN MIX IT WITH THE SALAD DRESSING IMMEDIATELY. BUY BANANA BLOSSOM AND PERILLA LEAF FROM THAI AND VIETNAMESE FOOD STORES.

CHICKEN & BANANA BLOSSOM SALAD

6 SERVES / STARTER

125 g (4½ oz) Chinese cabbage (wongbok)
500 g (1 lb 2 oz) shredded cooked chicken
90 g (3¼ oz/1 cup) bean sprouts
½ small white onion, sliced into fine rings
1 large handful of Vietnamese mint leaves
1 small handful of mint leaves
1 small handful of perilla leaves
4 kaffir lime (makrut) leaves

1 small banana blossom
125 ml (4 fl oz/½ cup) nuoc mam cham (page 180)
40 g (1½ oz/¼ cup) roasted peanuts, chopped
20 g (¾ oz/¼ cup) fried Asian shallots
1 bird's eye chilli, finely sliced

Slice the cabbage as finely as you can, wash it well, then place in a colander and leave to dry. Place the cabbage, chicken, bean sprouts and onion rings in a large mixing bowl. Roughly chop the Vietnamese mint, mint and perilla, then finely slice the lime leaves and add all the herbs to the bowl.

Peel and discard the dark red leaves of the banana blossom until you reach the tender white leaves inside. Place the white banana blossom on a chopping board and cut off 5 mm (¼ inch) from both the bottom and top of the blossom (this makes it easier to peel). Quickly peel and separate the tender white leaves. The little finger-like objects in between the leaves are the juvenile bananas — don't mix these into your salad, as they taste soapy and dry. Lay the white leaves on top of each other and, using a very sharp knife, cut across the leaf as finely as you can.

Mix the blossom through your salad and immediately dress it with the nuoc mam cham. Toss to combine and serve either individually or in one large serving bowl, garnished with the peanuts, fried shallots and chilli.

MY VERSION OF COQ AU VIN

4 SERVES / MAIN

1 x 1.8 kg (4 lb) chicken
60 g (2¼ oz) butter
150 g (5½ oz) speck or bacon
400 g (14 oz) French shallots, peeled
300 g (10½ oz) button mushrooms, cleaned
4 garlic cloves, finely chopped

1 tablespoon plain (all-purpose) flour
500 ml (17 fl oz/2 cups) red wine
2 bay leaves
¼ bunch of thyme
1 bunch of parsley stalks
1 tablespoon chopped parsley

Wash the chicken inside and out under cold running water, then pat dry with paper towel. With a sharp knife, cut the legs off the chicken and then separate the drumstick from the thigh. Cut the thigh in half across the middle of the thighbone. Using kitchen scissors, remove the cage (ribs and backbone) of the chicken. Cut the breast through the middle to separate them, leaving the meat attached to the breastbone. Remove the wings, then cut each breast into three pieces.

Place a large deep-sided frying pan over medium–high heat. Add 20 g (¾ oz) of the butter, the speck, shallots and mushrooms and cook for 3 minutes, then add the garlic and cook for a further 2 minutes, or until the shallots are golden. Remove the ingredients from the pan and place in a bowl.

Wipe the frying pan clean with paper towel, then add the remaining butter and fry the chicken pieces, skin side down, over medium heat until golden brown. Turn the chicken over. Sprinkle the flour over the chicken and stir to coat.

Deglaze the bottom of the pan by adding the wine and using a wooden spoon to scrape off any caramelised bits. Return the speck, shallots, mushrooms and garlic to the pan. Tie the bay leaves, thyme and parsley stalks together with some kitchen string and put in the frying pan. Reduce the heat, then cover the pan and simmer for about 45 minutes, or until the chicken is tender and cooked through. Remove the herbs and season the sauce with sea salt and freshly ground black pepper. Arrange the chicken on a platter, pour the sauce over and garnish with the parsley.

CHICKEN POT-ROASTED WITH HERBS & GARLIC

4 SERVES / MAIN

1 x 1.8 kg (4 lb) chicken
1 garlic bulb
50 g (1¾ oz) butter
2 carrots, cut into 5 mm (¼ inch) dice
3 onions, cut into 5 mm (¼ inch) dice
500 ml (17 fl oz/2 cups) white wine

2 litres (70 fl oz/8 cups) chicken stock
¼ bunch of thyme
¼ bunch of sage
¼ bunch of rosemary
2 bay leaves

Wash the chicken inside and out under cold running water, then pat dry with paper towel. Place a kitchen cloth over the garlic bulb and give it a whack with a meat mallet; this should separate the cloves. Peel off the skin, leaving the cloves whole.

Place a cast-iron casserole pot over medium heat and add the butter. Add the chicken and seal it on all sides until the skin is golden brown. Remove the chicken from the pot and set aside. Pour off all but 3 tablespoons of fat from the pot. Return the pot to the heat and fry the garlic, carrot and onion for about 5 minutes, or until they are golden brown. Deglaze the bottom of the pot by adding the wine and using a wooden spoon to scrape off any caramelised bits of vegetable and chicken.

Return the chicken to the pot, breast side up. Reduce the wine by half, then add the stock and bring to the boil. Add the herbs, then reduce the heat and simmer, covered, for 45 minutes, or until the chicken is very tender. Season to taste with sea salt and freshly ground black pepper.

DEPENDING ON THE SEASON, YOU COULD SERVE THIS DISH WITH OTHER VEGETABLES COOKED IN THE SAME POT AS THE CHICKEN – GREEN BEANS, PEAS, BRUSSELS SPROUTS OR MUSHROOMS.

A GOOD MARINADE IS CREATED TO ENHANCE RATHER THAN SMOTHER THE FLAVOUR OF THE MEAT. AT FIRST GLANCE, THE INGREDIENTS IN THIS MARINADE APPEAR QUITE ROBUST AND BOLD, BUT I THINK I HAVE SUCCEEDED IN FINDING THE RIGHT BALANCE.

CHICKEN ROASTED WITH LEMONGRASS, CHILLI & GARLIC

4 SERVES / MAIN

1 x 1.8 kg (4 lb) chicken
125 ml (4 fl oz/½ cup) nuoc mam cham, to serve (page 180)

MARINADE
2 lemongrass stems, white part only, finely sliced (reserve the green top part)
6 spring onions (scallions), white part only, finely sliced

4 garlic cloves, finely chopped
1 teaspoon minced pickled red chilli
3 tablespoons fish sauce
3 tablespoons coconut oil
1 tablespoon honey
2 teaspoons caster (superfine) sugar

Wash the chicken inside and out under cold running water, then pat dry with paper towel. Mix all of the marinade ingredients together, stirring until the sugar has dissolved and is well combined. Rub the chicken inside and out with the marinade. Place the chicken in a bowl and marinate in the fridge for at least 2 hours, or preferably overnight, before roasting.

Preheat the oven to 180°C (350°F/Gas 4). Put the reserved green tops of the lemongrass in a baking dish. Place the chicken, breast side up, on top of the lemongrass and roast for 20 minutes, then turn the chicken on its side and roast for another 20 minutes. Repeat the process on the other side, roasting for a further 20 minutes until the juices from the thickest part of the thigh run clear when pierced with a fork.

Once cooked, allow the chicken to rest for 10 minutes, then cut it in half from front to back. Separate the breast from the thigh, then use a cleaver to cut the meat through the bone into 1 cm (½ inch) pieces. Serve with steamed rice and nuoc mam cham for dipping.

GRILLED SPATCHCOCK WITH GARLIC, CHILLI & SPRING ONION

4 SERVES / MAIN

4 x 500 g (1 lb 2 oz) spatchcocks
   (poussins)
8 garlic cloves, finely chopped
2 long red chillies, finely chopped
6 small red chillies, finely chopped
12 spring onions (scallions), white part
   bashed with the back of a knife (slice
   some of the green tops for garnish)

2 teaspoons sea salt
¼ teaspoon white pepper
finely grated zest and juice of 2 lemons
200 ml (7 fl oz) olive oil
100 g (3½ oz) butter, at room
   temperature

Using kitchen scissors, cut the spatchcock along its backbone from the back to the front. Gently open the spatchcock up, turn it over and lay it on a chopping board, bone side down. Press down on the spatchcock to splay it flat. Repeat for the other spatchcocks. Wash the spatchcocks under cold running water, then pat dry with paper towel.

To make the marinade, place the garlic, chillies, white part of the spring onion, sea salt and white pepper in a mortar. Bash to combine the ingredients, then stir through the lemon zest and juice and olive oil. Place the spatchcocks in a large non-reactive mixing bowl and rub well with the marinade. Refrigerate for 2 hours, or overnight for the best result.

Remove the spatchcocks from the marinade and wipe off the excess. Place the marinade in a small saucepan over medium heat and bring to the boil. Continue to boil for 2 minutes, then add the butter and stir to combine. Remove the pan from the heat.

The spatchcocks are best cooked over charcoal but good results can be achieved by using a gas barbecue. Preheat your barbecue grill to medium–high. Place the spatchcocks, skin side down, on the barbecue and grill for 3 minutes, basting them constantly with the marinade. Pick them up and give them a quarter turn, place them skin side down again, and cook for another 3 minutes. Turn the spatchcocks over and repeat the cooking process, but this time you may need to cook them for 5–6 minutes before turning. To see if they are cooked, prick the leg with a fork — the juice should run clear. Scatter the spring onion greens over the spatchcocks and serve.

161

PORK

CONTENTS

& LAMB '163

PORK

IN MARCH 2009, UNDER THE COVER OF DARKNESS, AN ANIMAL ACTIVIST ILLEGALLY ENTERED THE GROUNDS OF AN INTENSIVE PIGGERY IN TASMANIA. WHAT SHE RECORDS ON FILM THAT NIGHT, AND LATER POSTS ON YOUTUBE, IS SOME OF THE MOST SHOCKING AND GRAPHIC FOOTAGE OF ANIMAL NEGLECT I HAVE EVER SEEN.

Walking with a video recorder in hand, we see through the lens of the camera the conditions on the ground at this particular piggery. On the door leading into the sow stalls is a sign proudly displaying the fact that the piggery is 'Australian quality pork accredited'. Inside the shed, we see what an alarming number of people who live in the city are too busy to acknowledge: animals continue to suffer in an intensive farm environment. The sow stalls, which are used to separate the pigs, are barely large enough to accommodate their ever-growing bodies. Standing there, bodies stained with excrement, their heads swing anxiously from side to side. Out of boredom they chew the metal bars that confine them. Many of the sows have infected and swollen legs, others have abscesses on their upper bodies, probably a result of constantly rubbing up against the bars. One pitiful creature, too weak to stand, lies in her own filth, her ribs protruding as she labours to breathe. Maggots wriggle under her skin as they eat away at the festering sores on her body. I can see the filth, and I am grateful I am not there to smell what must be a stomach-turning stench. These animals are obviously and outrageously mistreated.

I cannot believe that in this day and age we don't treat the animals within our food production system with respect! My anger was further compounded when I learnt this particular piggery supplied meat to one of our biggest supermarket chains. At first I wasn't sure how to react and express my outrage. Pigs are one of my favourite animals and pork is my favourite meat. As angry and repulsed as I was, I knew this video would not turn me off eating it.

After watching the video, with the images still fresh in my mind, I went to my local butcher and bought organic pork cutlets for dinner. You may find this odd, but because I only buy free-range or organic pork, every time I shop I cast a vote against the intensive pork industry. If only everyone did the same. I am confident that farmers who raise pigs organically or free-range do so because they care about the welfare of their animals and nurture the environment in which they live. I was so determined not to let the actions of one ignorant farmer dissuade me from eating the meat I love. I will always support people with an ethical backbone no matter what their field of endeavour.

Most of us care about the rights of animals, but often this isn't enough to motivate us into action. I am grateful someone had the courage to make this film and expose the conditions in this piggery to the world. The company and the farmer were eventually taken to court and fined for animal cruelty. This farmer no longer operates a piggery, but I wonder if this was an isolated case? I'd like to believe so, but am I kidding myself? Australia is renowned for following some of the best farm practice in the world. I think this is why I was so infuriated and disappointed when I first saw that footage.

We, as urban consumers of farm produce, have no choice but to trust the people who produce our food. Living in the city, we rarely meet the farmer who grows, or produces, our food, although farmers' markets are now blossoming and challenging this idea. Most

of us buy produce from our local shopping strip or supermarket. We place our trust in the different bodies that regulate farm practice. You would think that a sign proclaiming 'Australian quality pork accredited' actually meant something but, unfortunately, as this case demonstrates, the system we trust to uphold animal welfare standards sometimes lets all concerned parties down.

The Australian pork industry has a code of practice legislated by Commonwealth and State governments. It seems, however, that it's one thing to legislate good farm practice and quite another to put people on the ground to enforce it. This farm seems to have operated under the government inspectors' radar and the office quite rightly came under scrutiny. When questioned, the inspectors blamed a chronic lack of funding and manpower as the reasons why farms that don't comply with regulations, such as this one, fall through the cracks.

When I was young, I can remember feeding the pigs on our friends' farm. These pigs led an idyllic life in comparison to intensively farmed animals. The twenty or so pigs weren't intensively housed together, but they weren't free to roam in a paddock either. They were kept in a large pen, built just off the back of the cow-milking shed, a common set-up for farmers with dairy cattle back then. Inside the pen there was a covered section for shelter as well as plenty of mud and hay to keep the pigs amused. The pigs ate grain and vegetable scraps, and every morning and night they would gorge themselves on fresh full-cream milk.

When we visited, it was our job to feed the milk to the pigs. This was simple enough; all we had to do was pour the milk into a trough. The difficult task was to ensure the smaller, less dominant pigs also received a fair share. Even with domesticated animals, it can be a daily struggle to survive. These were definitely happy pigs, well fed and very active. They had room to move, straw to toss and play with, and a muddy wallow to keep them cool. But at the end of the day, they were being raised for their meat, and after 6 to 10 months they were headed to the same place as those raised on an intensive farm. If the two were to meet at the abattoir, I wonder which one would be more content with the life they had lived?

Pigs are sentient animals that some scientists credit with the intelligence of a three-year-old child. I know from experience they are extremely perceptive. When the pigs I helped raise were ready for market, a contract driver would turn up in a truck and reverse it up to the pen. This would cause a huge commotion; it was as if the sows had learnt the link between the arrival of the truck and the disappearance of their offspring. I observed this behaviour in pigs that had led a fairly charmed life. I can only imagine the anxiety and confusion suffered by pigs raised within an intensive system.

INTENSIVELY FARMED PIGS

In the 1950s pigs started to be moved off the land and into intensive farming systems. Effectively, they went from being an outdoor animal with the freedom to exercise their innate behaviours, to an indoor animal, confined and restricted. During this time the whole philosophy of farming was undergoing major change. A new farming model was being implemented, one that would see a greater emphasis placed on farm efficiency and production volume. Around the same time the chicken industry underwent a similar unfortunate transformation. Many similarities still exist between the two — both focus on producing and selling a high volume of meat protein for the cheapest possible price.

A minimum code of practice exists to protect animals within our agricultural system. Unfortunately, especially for intensively raised animals, I don't believe these standards offer satisfactory protection. In fact, many people argue that living conditions for pigs inside intensive farms are cruel and inhumane. For me, the most inhumane farm practice occurs long before the pigs destined for the table are even born — the practice of confining sows in stalls.

Here's a brief overview of the life cycle of the pigs on an intensive farm. After the sows are impregnated, they are isolated and confined to stalls for the period of their gestation, and are then moved into farrowing crates to give birth. The piglets stay with their mothers for 4 to 6 weeks. After this time they are transferred to pens with other pigs, and are grown out until they reach market weight.

A summary of the code of practice for pigs raised on an intensive farm states that pigs must have access to food and water, must be free from discomfort, pain, injury and disease, and live free from stress and fear. In all likelihood, the piglets that are born and then raised for their meat (weaners) experience some benefit from these codes, but what about Mum?

Although the code states that pigs must be free from pain and discomfort, it is hard to see how this is put into practice. Minimum dimensions exist for the size and construction of the stalls, but these dimensions only allow the sows to move slightly forwards and backwards; there is no room to turn around.

Pigs are social and intelligent creatures. They must be able to see one another and have some level of social interaction. Although the pigs can see each other from their position in the stalls, the only stimulation most of them get is when they bite each other through the bars. It is common for pigs to have their tails docked and teeth clipped to limit the damage they can inflict on one other. With nothing to keep their minds active and in the absence of organic material to play with, many pigs chew at the metal bars to pass the time.

The farrowing crates the sows are moved to are supposedly designed to protect the piglets from getting crushed when their mother suddenly decides to lie down. A steel barrier supports the weight of the sow as she lowers herself to the ground, giving the piglets time to escape from under her. I can appreciate the logic behind this, but evidence suggests the survival rate of piglets born inside a farrowing crate is similar to that of piglets born outside one. So why are they still used?

This question provokes a passionate debate between supporters and non-supporters of the practice. If a farmer has always used farrowing crates successfully and perceives they cause no harm to the pigs, then why change? Familiarity breeds content, I suppose. On the other side, farmers who have a more holistic approach to farming have never seen the need for them. In the near future, I believe sow stalls and farrowing crates will become obsolete. The Tasmanian government has agreed to phase out sow stalls starting in 2014, and it is only a matter of time before the other states address this issue.

It appears the only code of practice that the sows do benefit from is that they receive regular meals and access to water. Both sows and weaners have access to ample food and water; in fact, the more they eat the faster they will grow. This seems to be the only code that operates to a maximum standard.

EFFECTIVE AND RESPONSIBLE DISPOSAL OF PIG
WASTE HAS ALWAYS BEEN A PROBLEM FOR THE
INDUSTRY, AS IT IS A MAJOR ENVIRONMENTAL
THREAT UNLESS PROPERLY TREATED. RECENTLY
THE INDUSTRY HAS STARTED TO LOOK AT THE
PROBLEM OF PIG WASTE DIFFERENTLY BY
CONVERTING WASTE INTO FERTILISER, AND
CAPTURING METHANE GAS AND USING IT TO RUN
PLANT EQUIPMENT. IT IS THIS SORT OF INNOVATIVE
THINKING THAT IS HELPING THE INDUSTRY
IMPROVE ITS ENVIRONMENTAL FOOTPRINT.

Creating a stress-free environment for pigs is possible. Pigs need stimulation and room to move. As I mentioned, they are social animals but occasionally show aggression to one another (the rationale behind isolating sows in stalls). The aggressive pigs need to be separated and isolated from the mob. To implement the necessary changes, farmers will have to incur additional labour and infrastructure costs. If consumers truly want the system to change and provide better outcomes for the pigs, they need to take this into account and be prepared to pay more for pork products. Individual farmers will not take action if the cost of changes comes at their end of the equation.

We have to move on from this notion of food being cheap. I can't stand the word being used to describe raw ingredients and produce. Produce that is truly nourishing and grown with integrity is seldom cheap; we pay a realistic price for its production, which represents good value for money. The real cost of cheap produce is hidden. Someone or something, usually the animals within the system, pay the real price of production. The modern intensively farmed pig is paying a huge price.

PIG BREEDS

The majority of pigs found in intensive piggeries owe their genetic make-up to three breeds: the Large White, Landrace and Duroc. These breeds have largish, long bodies (good for bacon), grow efficiently and have good-sized litters. Regrettably, given the role biodiversity plays towards the survival of a species, they represent just three of the 73 breeds that exist in the world today. Sadly, a breed that is valued and deemed important one day is not necessarily so the next. A good example of this is the rise and fall, and rise again, of the Duroc. In 1922, the first Duroc pigs were imported into Australia from America. By 1936 they had gained popularity with local producers and were highly prized, but by 1940, just a few years later, the breed had become extinct in this country. This is how quickly trends and sentiment for specific breeds can change. It was 40 years before the Australian pork industry showed interest in the Duroc breed again, importing them this time from Canada and New Zealand. However, it's not just wild animals and rare breeds that are under threat of extinction; many domesticated animals face the same threat, too. There are approximately 4500 different breeds of domesticated animals left in the world. Frighteningly, we are losing approximately two breeds every week.

At culinary school I was taught to recognise the quality points of a piece of pork, but the breed and provenance of the pig were never discussed. Today the dialogue is changing, as more and more people demand to know how their pork is produced. I have friends who are so against the intensively raised pork industry they have given up pork altogether. I commend them for their stand, but not all pork comes from pigs raised on intensive farms. Recently, there has been a dynamic resurgence and interest in rare breeds of pigs, breeds that are now raised more humanely on free-range or organic farms. Today when chefs talk about pork, we not only talk about the quality points of pork, we also discuss these prized rare breeds such as Berkshire, Wessex Saddlebacks, Tamworth and Large Black and how they are raised.

Because these rare breeds aren't suited to indoor intensive production, the pork industry boffins decided they were no longer viable and consequently many breeds were forgotten; some faced the danger of extinction. Fortunately, the majority of rare breeds managed to escape this fate and have gone on to become the 'heroes' of modern-day cuisine. The meat from these pigs is so good, so full of fat and flavour that it is the only pork I use. But if they are so rare, why am I — and more and more chefs like me — using them? Ironically, to save their bacon, so to speak, we need to eat more of them. We are telling these farmers that we value their pork and appreciate the pigs they produce — if they continue to breed and nurture them, we will buy them. It is a simple economic equation but one that might just hold the key to the survival of the rare-breed pigs.

FREE-RANGE AND ORGANIC FARMS

Free-range and organic farmers are also bound by the same code of practice that is in place for intensive farmers. Whereas most intensive farmers seem to adhere more obviously to the code of unrestricted access to fresh food and water, free-range and organic farmers ensure the other requirements on the list are also met.

For me to present a slightly more balanced overview of the pork industry, it is important to note that there are different levels of compliance to the codes within the free-range pork industry, just as there are within the intensive system.

The term 'free-range' is confusing in itself, especially when applied to the labelling of pork products at the retail level. Pork products can be legally labelled as free-range even though the pig that provided the meat may not have ever foraged in a paddock or on open range. Sows are free to forage on open range, but once the piglets are born and weaned, they are then raised in huts. The piglets live an undeniably better life in the huts than they would on an intensive farm, but at no stage in their life do they live outdoors and forage on open range. The pork from these pigs is labelled as 'born free-range'. This is in contrast to a true free-range pig, which is born and lives on open pasture.

Free-range pigs live in paddocks in social groups, and are protected from predators. Specially designed shelters keep the pigs dry and warm; inside, the pigs make straw nests to sleep on. The shelters are either fixed in one position or can be moved into different locations around the paddock. The pigs are virtually unrestricted, free to exercise their natural tendencies, root around in the dirt and wallow in the mud to keep cool. The intensive pork industry is keen to point out it is inhumane to raise pigs outdoors because of their susceptibility to heat stress. (Pigs in intensive piggeries are usually raised in air-conditioned sheds.) This is a valid point, so free-range pigs tend to be raised in temperate climates.

The farmer who raises the free-range Kurobuta Berkshire pigs I use in the restaurant has a slightly different approach. His piglets are born to sows that live free-range. After they are weaned, the piglets live in a hut until they reach a certain size. When the piglets are big and healthy enough to fend off potential predators — usually after 4 weeks — they are reintroduced to the open range, where they remain until it is time for processing.

True free-range producers are trying to change the labelling laws. They, as do I, believe the average consumer doesn't know the difference between the two. 'Born free-range' farmers are getting the same price and ethical advantages even though their pigs aren't completely free-range. True free-range farmers should get the acknowledgement they deserve and the financial benefits of a complete free-range system.

ANTIBIOTICS AND HORMONES

Free-range pigs are free from antibiotic and growth hormones. Rules for organically raised pigs are even more stringent and are governed by an independent certifying body. Organic pigs can only be raised on pasture that is certified free of herbicides and pesticides. Naturally, the pigs can only eat grain that is certified organic. As I stated in the poultry chapter, not all free-range producers, even though they operate their farms to exceptional standards, apply for organic certification. This is why it is so important to ask your butcher where and how the pork he sells is produced.

THE FUTURE FOR THE INDUSTRY

Climate change will present major challenges for both the intensive and free-range pork industries. To keep costs down, intensive piggeries are typically located close to areas that grow grain crops. Future erratic weather conditions are predicted to affect the growing capacity and availability of these crops, and will put upward pressure on the price of grain. Rising temperatures will also affect the general health of the pigs — pigs can't regulate their own body temperature so often suffer heat stress. Intensive piggeries already use air-conditioning to keep pigs cool, so any rise in temperature is likely to hit free-range farmers hardest.

I have met farmers who raise pigs in the intensive farming system who are every bit as passionate about what they do as farmers who raise pigs free-range or organically. In most cases, intensive farmers strive to achieve the best possible outcomes for their pigs. If we manage to take the sow stalls and farrowing crates out of the equation, the conditions for the animals in their care would be vastly improved. There is no doubt that an intensive piggery operation creates an artificial environment, but it is an environment that can be totally controlled. Climate change will bring new challenges; hypothetically, a controlled environment might very well be the answer the industry needs to operate responsibly into the future. It is a complex problem to solve. But while the intensive pig farming industry continues to operate as it does today, I will continue to support the farmers who produce free-range pigs.

LAMB

THE DAYS OF AUSTRALIA LIVING OFF THE SHEEP'S BACK ARE
WELL AND TRULY OVER. THE ORIGINAL EXPRESSION SEEMS TO
HAVE STOOD THE TEST OF TIME, BUT UNFORTUNATELY TODAY
THE INDUSTRY'S CONTRIBUTION TO THE NATIONAL ECONOMY
IS NOTHING LIKE IT WAS IN ITS HEYDAY AT THE TURN OF THE
TWENTIETH CENTURY. DESPITE THIS, MOST AUSTRALIANS STILL
REMEMBER THE KEY ROLE THE INDUSTRY PLAYED IN AUSTRALIA'S
EARLY AGRICULTURAL DEVELOPMENT. THE ANNUAL AUSTRALIA
DAY LAMB MARKETING CAMPAIGNS ENCOURAGE US TO EAT LAMB,
AND IF WE DON'T ... WELL, WE ARE SIMPLY UN-AUSTRALIAN.

On Australia Day, the aroma of lamb cooking in the backyards and kitchens of suburban homes pervades the air and our consciousness. Lamb recipes are now too numerous to be counted, and reflect the breadth of Australia's cultural diversity. Some of my favourites include lamb mince wok-tossed with sweet soy sauce; backstrap chargrilled with lemon, yoghurt and mint; breast stuffed, rolled and roasted with spiced burghul; and my partner Pauline's favourite, pan-fried loin chops marinated in preserved bean curd paste. The list of ingredients that complement the flavour of lamb are as abundant as our sense of gratitude to the early pioneers of the industry. Today, lamb is such an inherent part of the national ethos it practically provides a metaphor for Australia's cultural unity. So how will the sheep and lamb industry, once so robust, weather the tide of climate and market uncertainty into the future?

To answer this question we have to first realise that it is impossible to separate the sheep from the lamb. By this I mean the sheep wool industry and the lamb meat industry are, essentially, the one industry. The first sheep introduced to Australia came with the First Fleet from the Cape of Good Hope. These were meat sheep — sheep covered with coarse hair, not cocooned in fine wool. For one reason or another they didn't fare well in the new colony. Later, Merino sheep, a breed originally from Spain, were introduced and they thrived. Merinos are large sheep renowned for their fine wool and for producing big 'meaty' lambs. Eighty per cent of the sheep in Australia today are descended from Merinos.

Merinos are routinely crossbred with British sheep breeds favoured for their meat quality, such as the Poll Dorset and Leicester. This crossbreeding creates a dual-purpose animal. In theory, sheep producers have a distinct advantage over producers of other terrestrial farm animals because they have two very different markets in which to sell their product — either the wool or meat market, depending on which has the greater demand and, subsequently, which will offer the greater return on their investment.

Sheep farmers, probably more so than their competitors, need the weather conditions to be reasonably predictable. Rain is always welcome, but if sheep farmers can get good winter rain, to encourage lush pasture growth, it almost guarantees a great spring. The lush pastures mean the ewes maintain condition, resulting in higher fertility and better than average lambing rates come springtime. When times are bad, farmers have to decide how best to manage their flock to profit from consumer demand. Do they keep more ewes for lamb production or more wethers for wool? They need to adjust the size and gender balance of their flock to best position themselves for when and if climatic conditions and the market change. This is always a gamble because once the decision is made it is not easily reversed.

In recent years, the crippling effects of drought have seen a steady decline in the total number of sheep in Australia. Unfortunately for the Australian sheep industry, during this same period the international demand for lamb meat has increased. Despite the fact there are fewer sheep, in a relatively short period of time farmers have managed to turn the national flock around so there now are more ewes (for lamb meat production) to take advantage of this demand. The fact that the industry now exports a greater quantity of meat from fewer lambs is a testament to the farmers' grit and determination. They have achieved this outcome by increasing the weight of the lambs at the time of slaughter.

I have had no experience raising sheep, however I have on many occasions observed them at close range. Over the years, my penchant for trout fishing has taken me through many sheep properties. Walking through the paddocks in the heat of summer, I tend to think about the same two things. One. Why am I walking through this dry paddock looking for a river to fly-fish for trout when it's over 30 degrees Celsius? Two. Why on earth do all these sheep look so healthy when the landscape is the colour of burnt clay, and there's not a blade of green grass in sight?

The answer to the first question is simple: trout fishing is an obsession, one fortunately lost on most sensible people. However, the answer to the second question tells us more about the constitution of the sheep themselves than the influence of good farm management. Sheep are predominately grass-fed and live extremely well on marginal land; land that is unsuitable for beef production. However, on the more fertile pastures of a mixed farm, sheep and cattle can co-exist, but it is the cattle that usually dominate the landscape. Sometimes cattle farmers who practise paddock rotation — where cattle graze in a paddock for a period of time before being moved on to the next, giving the first paddock time to rest and regenerate — have sheep follow the cattle through the paddock to clean up or eat the weeds left behind. Other farmers would never do this because they believe the sheep eat the perennial grasses down too close to the roots, slowing the regeneration process. Either way, one thing is certain: sheep will eat practically anything, and left unmanaged this can have disastrous effects on the environment.

In times of good rainfall and average temperatures, nature can usually stay abreast of grazing pressure. However, during periods of continuous drought, nature's resilience is seriously challenged. Climate change is forecast to exaggerate the extremes of Australia's weather conditions, with a greater occurrence, and longer periods, of drought. Large areas of Australia are already overgrazed and the salinity of the soil is such that it will no longer sustain vegetation. As the earth bakes and rainfall declines, sheep will have an even greater impact on the land. Rising temperatures and heat stress will also directly affect the sheep, resulting in a decrease of overall lamb production. Not only will there be fewer lambs, but their growth rate will be hampered, too. Sheep eat less in times of extreme heat and therefore convert less food into body mass.

Climate change will reduce the amount of land suitable for sheep grazing. However, the increase in carbon dioxide in the atmosphere is expected to accelerate the growth of fodder crops, but unfortunately the nutritional value of these crops is expected to fall, negating any benefit. When this happens, the whole dynamic of the industry will change: sheep may need to be moved off the land and into feedlots. At present, over 90 per cent of all sheep are raised on grass, and during 2008 and 2009 only 7 per cent of all lamb produced for meat were fed grain, on average for a period of 59 days. The feeding of sheep in feedlots is not yet a real animal welfare concern — but in the future? Today, the more important welfare issues centre on the live-sheep export trade, and particularly relate to the holding of animals in pens prior to them being shipped overseas and the conditions on board during transportation.

The sheep industry will face many challenges in the future and it will need to find clever solutions to maintain or increase production. Agricultural industries will compete more aggressively with each other for basic resources and for our shopping dollar. At present, the majority of sheep are grass-fed and convert the energy into body mass quite efficiently. If sheep are moved into feedlots, the need for fodder crops and grain will place increasing pressure on land, water and energy resources. When this happens, it will throw a whole new range of ethical and sustainability questions into the arena. But, until then, I try to cook ethically and sustainably by using less popular cuts of lamb such as the neck, shoulder and breast, served, as per my general belief, in small proportion with plenty of garden-fresh vegetables.

ASIAN-STYLE SPICY PORK MINCE SALAD

4 SERVES / STARTER

2 tablespoons vegetable oil
1 lemongrass, white part only, finely
   chopped
2 garlic cloves, finely chopped
400 g (14 oz) minced (ground) pork
a pinch of salt and white pepper
2 Chinese cabbage (wongbok) leaves,
   finely shredded
2 iceberg lettuce leaves, finely shredded

1 large handful of snow pea (mangetout)
   shoots
½ red onion, finely sliced
10 Thai basil leaves
10 spearmint leaves
10 coriander (cilantro) leaves
2 bird's eye chillies, sliced
1 quantity nuoc mam cham (recipe below)
2 tablespoons crushed roasted peanuts

Place a wok or large frying pan over medium heat. Add the oil and fry the lemongrass until it starts to colour, then add the garlic and continue to cook until the lemongrass is light brown and the garlic is golden. Increase the heat, add the pork mince and toss and stir the ingredients to combine the flavours. Cook the pork until golden brown, season with the salt and white pepper and set aside to cool.

   Place the cabbage, lettuce, snow pea shoots, onion, herbs and chilli in a mixing bowl. Add the pork and half the nuoc mam cham and mix well. Set aside to marinate for 2 minutes, then transfer to a serving platter and garnish with the peanuts. Add more dressing if you like.

NUOC MAM CHAM MAKES 250 ML (9 FL OZ/1 CUP)

3 tablespoons fish sauce
3 tablespoons rice vinegar
2 tablespoons caster (superfine) sugar

2 tablespoons lime juice
2 garlic cloves, finely chopped
1 bird's eye chilli, finely diced

Put the fish sauce, vinegar, sugar and 125 ml (4 fl oz/½ cup) of water in a saucepan. Mix well to dissolve the sugar, then place the pan over high heat and bring to the boil. Once boiled, remove the pan from the heat and allow to cool. Add the lime juice, garlic and chilli to the dressing and stir to combine.

WHENEVER A RECIPE REQUIRES
PORK MINCE I ASK MY BUTCHER
TO MINCE A PIECE OF FREE-
RANGE PORK NECK. I FIND IT HAS
THE RIGHT BALANCE OF FAT
AND LEAN MEAT.

THE FAT IS AN INTEGRAL PART OF THIS ROAST PORK EXPERIENCE. IT'S CRAZY TO THINK THE MODERN PIG HAS BEEN BRED TO CONTAIN LESS FAT. IT IS SUCH A PLEASURE TO SLICE AND EAT JUST-ROASTED PORK WITH YOUR HANDS, LETTING THE FAT RUN DOWN YOUR ARMS.

ROASTED PORK SHOULDER SERVED WITH LEMON, SALT & PEPPER

8 SERVES / MAIN

150 ml (5 fl oz) light soy sauce
100 ml (3½ fl oz) shaoxing rice wine
3 garlic cloves, sliced
5 cm (2 inch) piece of ginger, peeled
   and sliced
2 kg (4 lb 8 oz) shoulder of pork, boned
   out, skin on

3 tablespoons sea salt
1 tablespoon sichuan peppercorns
2 large onions, cut in half with the
   skin on
1 lemon, halved

To make a marinade for the pork, mix the soy sauce, rice wine, garlic and ginger in a bowl. Score the pork skin at 1 cm (½ inch) intervals. Place the pork in a clean food-grade plastic bag, then pour the marinade into the bag and seal. Rub the outside of the bag to coat the pork evenly with the marinade. Place in the fridge to marinate overnight, skin side facing up.

To make sichuan salt and pepper, dry-roast the sea salt and sichuan peppercorns in a heavy-based frying pan. Roast until the peppercorns begin to pop and become aromatic, then tip the salt and pepper into a bowl. Allow to cool, then grind into a fine powder using a mortar and pestle.

Preheat the oven to 200°C (400°F/Gas 6). Place the halved onions, flat side down, in a roasting tin. Lay the pork, skin side up, over the onions. Pour any marinade left in the plastic bag over the pork. Roast in the oven for 1 hour, or until the pork is cooked through and the skin is a deep golden brown. Remove from the oven, cover and rest in a warm place for 30 minutes. To serve, squeeze the lemon juice over the pork, season with the sichuan salt and pepper, and slice.

ENGLISH-STYLE PORK PIE WITH A HINT OF SPICE

8 SERVES / MAIN OR LUNCH DISH

PASTRY

560 g (1 lb 4 oz/3¾ cups) plain
  (all-purpose) flour, sifted
225 g (8 oz) butter, diced
¾ teaspoon salt
130 g (4½ oz) egg yolks (6–7 yolks)
90 ml (3 fl oz) cold water
1 egg, lightly beaten with 1 tablespoon milk

1.5 kg (3 lb 5 oz) boneless pork leg, skin on
50 g (1¾ oz) butter

250 g (9 oz) onions, finely sliced
250 g (9 oz) pork belly, minced (ground)
250 g (9 oz) pancetta or smoky bacon,
  rind removed, chopped
2 garlic cloves, finely sliced
4 thyme sprigs, leaves finely chopped
1 tablespoon ground fennel
2 teaspoons ground coriander
1 teaspoon salt
1 teaspoon white pepper
100 ml (3½ fl oz) sweet sherry

To make the pastry, put the flour, butter and salt in a food processor and pulse for 15 seconds. Add the egg yolks one at a time, and pulse for a few seconds after adding each yolk. With the motor running, slowly pour in the water until the dough comes together. Turn the dough out onto a lightly floured work surface and knead into a ball. Flatten the dough, wrap it in plastic wrap and rest it in the fridge for 1 hour.

To make the filling, trim the pork leg of skin and fat and cut into 2 cm (¾ inch) cubes — you should yield 1 kg (2 lb 4 oz) of meat. Place the butter in a saucepan over medium heat, add the onions and cook slowly for 10–15 minutes, stirring occasionally, until the onions are caramelised. Set aside to cool. In a bowl, place the pork belly, pancetta, garlic, thyme, spices, salt and white pepper and loosely mix together. Add the sherry and mix to incorporate the flavours. Stir in the onions when cool. Set aside while you prepare the pastry shell.

You will need a 20 cm (8 inch) non-stick spring-form cake tin. Remove the dough from the fridge and rest it at room temperature for 15 minutes. Cut off a quarter of the dough and set it aside for the lid. Flour the work surface and gently roll out the remaining dough to a 1 cm (½ inch) thickness, with a diameter of 30 cm (12 inches). Line the tin with the dough, pressing it into the bottom edge and over the top of the tin, then chill in the fridge for 15 minutes. Meanwhile, roll out the dough for the lid and leave it at room temperature.

Fill the pie base with the pork filling, pressing it down firmly into the base. Brush the top of the pie with the egg wash, then lay the lid on top. Secure the top of the pie to the bottom by crimping the edges together well to seal. Make a small crisscross incision in the centre of the pie lid and brush the top with egg wash. Place in the fridge for 20 minutes.

Preheat the oven to 160°C (315°F/Gas 2–3). Place the pie on the middle rack in the oven and cook for 1½ hours, then increase the heat to 200°C (400°F/Gas 6) to brown the top, if necessary. Once the top is browned, remove the pie from the oven. Allow it to cool on a wire rack to room temperature, then refrigerate until cold. Remove from the tin, slice and serve.

PORK LEG IS QUITE LEAN BUT THE
ADDITION OF PORK BELLY IN THIS
RECIPE HELPS KEEP THE FILLING
MOIST. THE PORK FAT IS SLOWLY
COOKED AND RENDERED THROUGH
THE PIE.

OVEN-ROASTED PORK CUTLETS WITH SWEET STICKY SAUCE

4 SERVES / MAIN

4 pork cutlets
1 garlic clove, sliced
250 ml (9 fl oz/1 cup) white wine
2 tablespoons olive oil

185 ml (6 fl oz/¾ cup) tomato sauce
(ketchup)
1 tablespoon sweet chilli sauce
250 ml (9 fl oz/1 cup) port

Put the pork cutlets, garlic, wine and some salt and freshly ground black pepper in a bowl. Mix well to coat the pork in the marinade, then place in the fridge and marinate for 1 hour.

Preheat the oven to 220°C (425°F/Gas 7). Remove the pork cutlets from the marinade and pat dry with paper towel. Remove and reserve the slices of garlic from the marinade. Place a frying pan over medium heat, add the olive oil and cook the pork for 3–4 minutes on each side, or until nicely browned. Place the pork in a roasting tin and season with sea salt and freshly ground black pepper.

Drain most of the fat from the frying pan, leaving 1 tablespoon. Return the pan to the heat, add the reserved garlic slices and cook for 2 minutes, then slowly add the tomato sauce, sweet chilli sauce and port. Bring to the boil and reduce the liquid by half. Pour the sauce over the cutlets in the roasting tin and place them in the oven. Cook for 8 minutes, then turn the pork over and cook for a further 8 minutes. Allow to rest for 10 minutes before serving.

BARBECUED PORK SPARERIBS COOKED IN CAPSICUM PASTE

4-6 SERVES / MAIN

ROASTED CAPSICUM PASTE
4 capsicums (peppers)
1 garlic bulb
3 tablespoons fish sauce
1 bird's eye chilli, chopped
good quality olive oil

2.5 kg (5 lb 8 oz) pork spareribs

To make the roasted capsicum paste, preheat the oven to 180°C (350°F/Gas 4). Place the capsicums and garlic bulb on a baking tray and roast for 30 minutes, or until the capsicum skins blacken and the garlic has completely softened. Remove the tray from the oven. Put the capsicums into an airtight container and allow them to sweat and cool slightly. Meanwhile, peel the garlic cloves and place the garlic flesh into a food processor. Remove the capsicums from the container and scrape away the blackened skin. Discard the skin, membrane and seeds, then put the capsicum flesh, fish sauce and chilli into the food processor with the garlic. Season with sea salt and freshly ground black pepper and process until smooth. Scrape the paste into a sterilised glass jar and then cover generously with olive oil. The capsicum paste can be stored in the fridge under the oil for up to 2 weeks.

Spread half the capsicum paste over the spareribs, reserving the remaining half for basting, and marinate for at least 1 hour and up to 4 hours.

Preheat the barbecue grill to medium. Cook the ribs for 10–15 minutes, basting them often with the reserved capsicum paste. Turn the ribs every 3 minutes or so until they are done, to prevent the marinade from burning.

THIS IS ONE OF MY FAVOURITE PORTUGUESE DISHES. TO SEE PORK AND SHELLFISH ON THE SAME PLATE IS NOT UNUSUAL; AT RED LANTERN OUR MENU HAS MANY EXAMPLES OF THIS PAIRING. PIPPIES ARE NOW MOSTLY SOLD ALREADY DEGORGED OF SAND, BUT IF IN DOUBT ASK YOUR FISHMONGER.

PORTUGUESE PORK BELLY WITH SHELLFISH

8 SERVES / MAIN

1 kg (2 lb 4 oz) piece of pork belly,
   skin removed, cut into 2.5 cm
   (1 inch) cubes
100 ml (3½ fl oz) dry white wine
500 ml (17 fl oz/2 cups) milk
4 bay leaves
3 tablespoons olive oil
8 French shallots, thinly sliced
4 garlic cloves, crushed

1 quantity roasted capsicum paste
   (page 187)
200 ml (7 fl oz) vermouth
350 ml (12 fl oz) chicken stock
1 bunch of thyme, picked
1.5 kg (3 lb 5 oz) pippies or clams (vongole)
   (free of sand and grit)
2 large handfuls of parsley, roughly
   chopped

Place the pork in a large bowl and add the wine, milk, bay leaves, a pinch of salt and a generous grind of black pepper. Place in the fridge and leave to marinate overnight.

Remove the pork from the marinade, rinse under cold running water, then pat dry with paper towel. Place a large flameproof casserole dish over high heat, add the olive oil, then fry the pork in small batches on all sides until it is a nice golden brown colour. Remove the pork as it colours and set it aside. Once all the pork is cooked, reduce the heat slightly and fry the shallots and garlic until they start to colour. Return the pork to the casserole dish with the capsicum paste and vermouth, and stir to combine the flavours. Bring the liquid to the boil, cover the dish, then reduce the heat so the liquid simmers very slowly, and continue to cook for 40 minutes.

Check that the pork is tender by inserting a skewer through the meat; it should pass through easily. Once cooked, increase the heat and add the chicken stock and thyme. When the liquid comes to the boil, add the shellfish, cover and cook for a further 5 minutes, or until the shellfish open. Discard any that remain closed. Check the broth for seasoning, then stir through the parsley. Serve with a side of kipfler potatoes.

PORK HOCK & BAKED HARICOT BEANS

4 SERVES / MAIN

2 tablespoons olive oil

200 g (7 oz) pancetta, cut into 2 cm
   (¾ inch) cubes

500 g (1 lb 2 oz) dried white haricot beans,
   soaked in plenty of cold water overnight

1 bay leaf

50 g (1¾ oz) soft brown sugar

3 tablespoons golden syrup or honey

1 tablespoon English mustard

8–10 baby onions

4 cloves

2 pork hocks

Place a flameproof casserole dish over medium heat, add the olive oil and fry the pancetta until slightly crisp. Drain the haricot beans and add them to the dish with the bay leaf and enough water to cover the beans by 5 cm (2 inches). Bring the beans to the boil, then reduce the heat and simmer gently for 1 hour. The beans should be just tender but not soft. Towards the end of cooking time, preheat the oven to 140°C (275°F/Gas 1).

Add the brown sugar, golden syrup and mustard to the casserole dish and stir to combine. Stud some of the onions with the cloves and add to the dish along with the pork hocks. Season with freshly ground black pepper and, if necessary, add enough water to cover the beans. Put the lid on the casserole dish, place it in the oven and cook for 2 hours. Remove the dish from the oven and gently stir the ingredients. Return the dish to the oven, without the lid, and cook for a further 1 hour. During this time the sauce will thicken and the meat should be falling from the bones. Remove the bones, stir, then check the seasoning. Serve with crusty bread.

PANCETTA, PROSCIUTTO AND MANY OTHER TRADITIONAL ITALIAN CURED MEATS ARE NOW MADE IN AUSTRALIA BY ARTISAN BUTCHERS. WHEN YOU BUY A PIECE OF PORK WITH THE BONE IN, YOU ARE SUPPORTING THE LOCAL PORK INDUSTRY. QUARANTINE LAWS PROHIBIT PORK BONES FROM ENTERING THE COUNTRY.

VIETNAMESE-STYLE FIVE-SPICE ROASTED PORK

6–8 SERVES / MAIN

3 spring onions (scallions), sliced
125 ml (4 fl oz/½ cup) shaoxing rice wine
3 tablespoons soy sauce
2 tablespoons hoisin sauce
2 tablespoons caster (superfine) sugar
2 tablespoons vegetable oil
2 kg (4 lb 8 oz) pork shoulder blade chops
1½ tablespoons Chinese five-spice

3 garlic cloves, finely chopped
4 cm (1½ inch) piece of ginger, finely
   chopped
1 teaspoon salt
½ teaspoon white pepper
coriander (cilantro) sprigs, to garnish
long red chilli, sliced, to garnish

Place the spring onions, rice wine, soy sauce, hoisin sauce, sugar, oil and 4 tablespoons water in a large bowl and mix well. Add the pork chops to the bowl, mix to coat well, then marinate overnight in the fridge.

Preheat the oven to 200°C (400°F/Gas 6). Remove the chops from the marinade and pat dry with paper towel, reserving the marinade for later use. Combine the five-spice, garlic, ginger, salt and white pepper. Rub the chops with the mixture, then leave the pork to marinate at room temperature for 30 minutes.

Meanwhile, put the reserved marinade in a saucepan over medium heat and reduce by half. Place a roasting tin (line it with foil to minimise washing up) on the bottom rack of the oven and place the pork chops directly on the oven racks over the tin. Cook the chops for 30 minutes, pulling the oven racks out slightly and basting the chops liberally with the reduced marinade every 10 minutes. (It can get a bit messy when you pull the oven racks out to baste the pork, so it's a good idea to lay an old kitchen cloth over the open oven door to catch the drips.)

Once cooked, remove the chops from the oven and allow to rest for 10 minutes. Place them on a serving platter and garnish with the coriander and chilli.

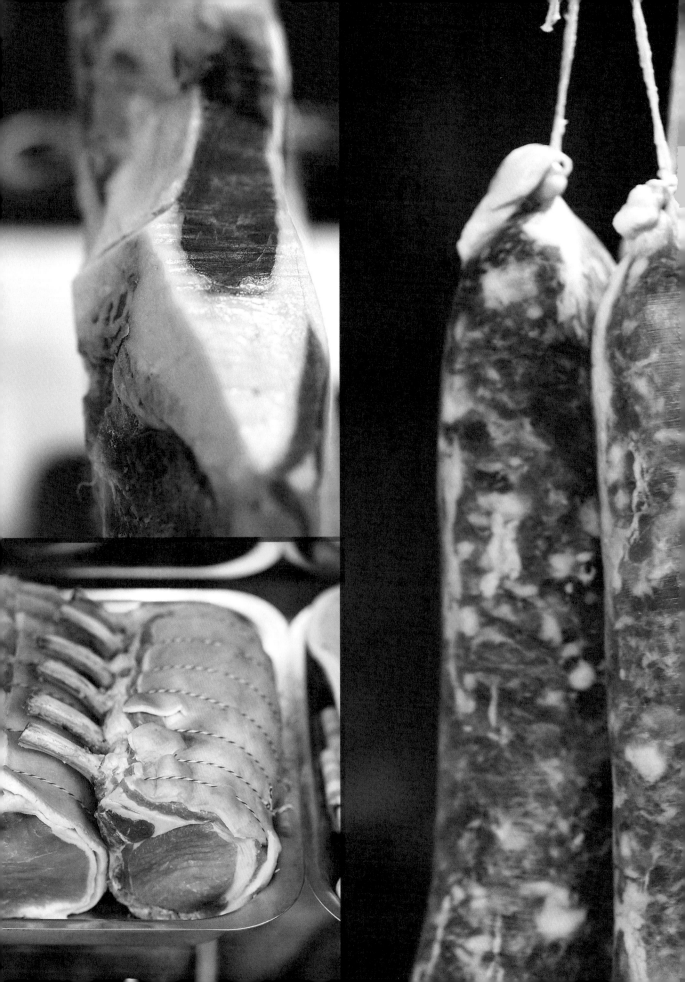

PORK FAT – FRIEND OR FOE?

EVERY WEEK, I USE A LARGE QUANTITY OF PORK IN MY RESTAURANT, RED LANTERN. ASIAN CULTURES LOVE PORK AND ASIAN CHEFS HAVE DEVELOPED A PLETHORA OF RECIPES FOR ITS PREPARATION. INTERESTINGLY, I FIND THE MOST DELICIOUS AND SUCCULENT ASIAN PORK RECIPES REQUIRE MEAT THAT IS FULL OF FAT. MY FAVOURITE CUTS OF PORK ARE THE BELLY, SHOULDER AND NECK, WHICH ALSO HAPPEN TO REPRESENT THE BEST VALUE. SLOWLY ROASTED OR BRAISED, THESE CUTS YIELD MEAT THAT IS STICKY AND UNCTUOUS, CREATING AN ADDICTIVE FEELING IN THE MOUTH THAT IS SECOND TO NONE. I DON'T KNOW WHY WE ARE SO SCARED OF FAT!

Today's intensively farmed pork has 16 per cent less fat and 27 per cent less saturated fat than it did 15 years ago. Consequently, most modern pork is fairly flavourless and unrewarding to eat. So, who made the decision to breed the fat out of intensively farmed pigs? We did! Over time the pork industry has interpreted market surveys and monitored our purchasing decisions, and whether we like to accept it or not, we are the ones who said 'no' to fat. So the industry responded and leaner pork is what we got.

Pork sales have historically been lower than other terrestrial-based meat products. To improve sales, and save the industry, something had to be done. The pork industry competes with the chicken, lamb and beef industries for our shopping dollar. In recent times, the industry has improved its market share considerably — pork is now perceived as a leaner and healthier meat alternative — but the industry still had to solve one problem: home cooks were having trouble cooking these new lean cuts of pork without it ending up like a dried-up old boot. The common misconception is that pork should be cooked right through, whereas it is best served pink. There is now very little fat left in pork to protect and moisten the meat during the cooking process. Cooking it right through removes all the moisture.

The industry jumped to its feet; there had to be a quick fix. But rather than reverse the cycle and breed pigs with more fat, they decided the best solution was to inject the pork with water to increase its moisture content. The more moisture in the pork to start with, the more moisture is retained after it is cooked. This works in theory but in practice I feel the texture and flavour of the meat is compromised.

We prepare pork dishes in the restaurant using Kurobuta Berkshire pork and our customers appreciate the full fatty flavour. When we chargrill pork loin chops we serve them pink. We have one customer who eats this dish every week and always asks for the juiciest pork chops we have — in other words, the chops with the most fat!

I SHOULDN'T TAKE CREDIT FOR THIS RECIPE; THIS ONE BELONGS TO MY PARTNER, PAULINE. SHE LOVES COOKING LAMB LOIN CHOPS THIS WAY. IF SHE HADN'T INTRODUCED IT TO ME, I NEVER WOULD HAVE SUSPECTED THAT LEMONGRASS WENT SO WELL WITH LAMB. YOU CAN MARINATE THE LAMB FOR AS LITTLE AS TWO HOURS IN THE LEMONGRASS, ALTHOUGH THE FLAVOUR IS TRULY ENHANCED WHEN YOU MARINATE IT OVERNIGHT.

PAULINE'S PAN-FRIED LAMB LOIN CHOPS WITH LEMONGRASS, CHILLI & GARLIC

4 SERVES / MAIN

4 lemongrass stems
4 garlic cloves
2–4 teaspoons minced pickled red
   chilli, to taste

4 tablespoons fish sauce
1 tablespoon caster (superfine) sugar
1 kg (2 lb 4 oz) lamb loin chops
2 tablespoons vegetable oil

Chop and throw away the bottom 1.5 cm (⅝ inch) of the lemongrass, then peel and discard the outer layers. Now finely chop the bottom tender 6 cm (2½ inches) or so of the stem and place it in a bowl. Finely chop the garlic and add it to the bowl along with the pickled chilli, fish sauce and sugar. Mix the ingredients well, then add the chops and marinate overnight.

To cook the chops, place a large frying pan over medium–high heat. Pour in the oil and swirl the pan to evenly distribute the oil around the pan. Cook the chops for about 3 minutes on each side for medium-rare, or cook to your liking.

I BELIEVE MEAT TASTES BETTER WHEN COOKED ON THE BONE. THE BONE PROTECTS AND KEEPS THE MEAT MOIST, AND THE LITTLE PIECES OF MEAT THAT CARAMELISE AROUND THE BONE ARE AN ADDED BONUS.

LAMB BREAST IS A FAIRLY INEXPENSIVE CUT TAKEN FROM THE
FOREQUARTER. YOU CAN BUY IT BONELESS BUT I PREFER TO BUY
IT WITH THE BONE IN. THE BONES CAN THEN BE USED AS A TRIVET
IN THE BOTTOM OF THE ROASTING TIN.

LAMB BREAST ROLLED & STUFFED WITH MINCE, PINE NUTS & CORIANDER

6 SERVES / MAIN

240 g (8 ½ oz/1⅓ cups) burghul
1 lamb breast, bone in (about 1.5 kg/
   3 lb 5 oz)
350 g (12 oz) minced (ground) lamb
1 large onion, finely diced
4 garlic cloves, crushed
1 tablespoon ground coriander
2 teaspoons ground cumin

1 teaspoon ground cinnamon
1 teaspoon cayenne pepper
1 bunch of coriander (cilantro), leaves
   finely chopped
100 g (3 ½ oz/⅔ cup) pine nuts, roughly
   chopped
finely grated zest of 2 lemons
olive oil

Soak the burghul in water for 1 hour. Take a handful of burghul at a time and squeeze out as much water as you can, placing the burghul in a clean bowl as you go.

Lay the lamb breast flat on a chopping board. Using the tip of a very sharp knife, carefully remove the breast bones from the meat, reserving the bones to use as a trivet. Removing the bones is very easily done, so don't be discouraged.

Preheat the oven to 160°C (315°F/Gas 2–3). Place the burghul, minced lamb, onion, garlic and all the spices into a food processor and process the mixture into a paste. Add the coriander, pine nuts and lemon zest and pulse to incorporate the ingredients.

Season the lamb breast with sea salt and then press the minced lamb mixture evenly over the surface of the breast, leaving 2.5 cm (1 inch) uncovered at the widest end. Pour a little olive oil over the mince and, starting from the narrow end, roll the breast up and secure with kitchen string. Rub a little more olive oil over the outside of the roll and season with sea salt.

Place the reserved lamb bones in a roasting tin, then place the lamb roll on top. Cook the lamb in the oven for 20 minutes, then reduce the heat to 140°C (275°F/Gas 1) and cook for another 2 hours. Remove the lamb from the oven and roll it up tightly in foil; leave it in a warm place for 15 minutes. If you like, an easy sauce can be made by deglazing the tin with a little white wine and chicken stock.

To serve, slice the lamb roll while it is still in the foil (this keeps the lamb neatly rolled). Place the lamb slices on the plates, then remove and discard the foil and kitchen string.

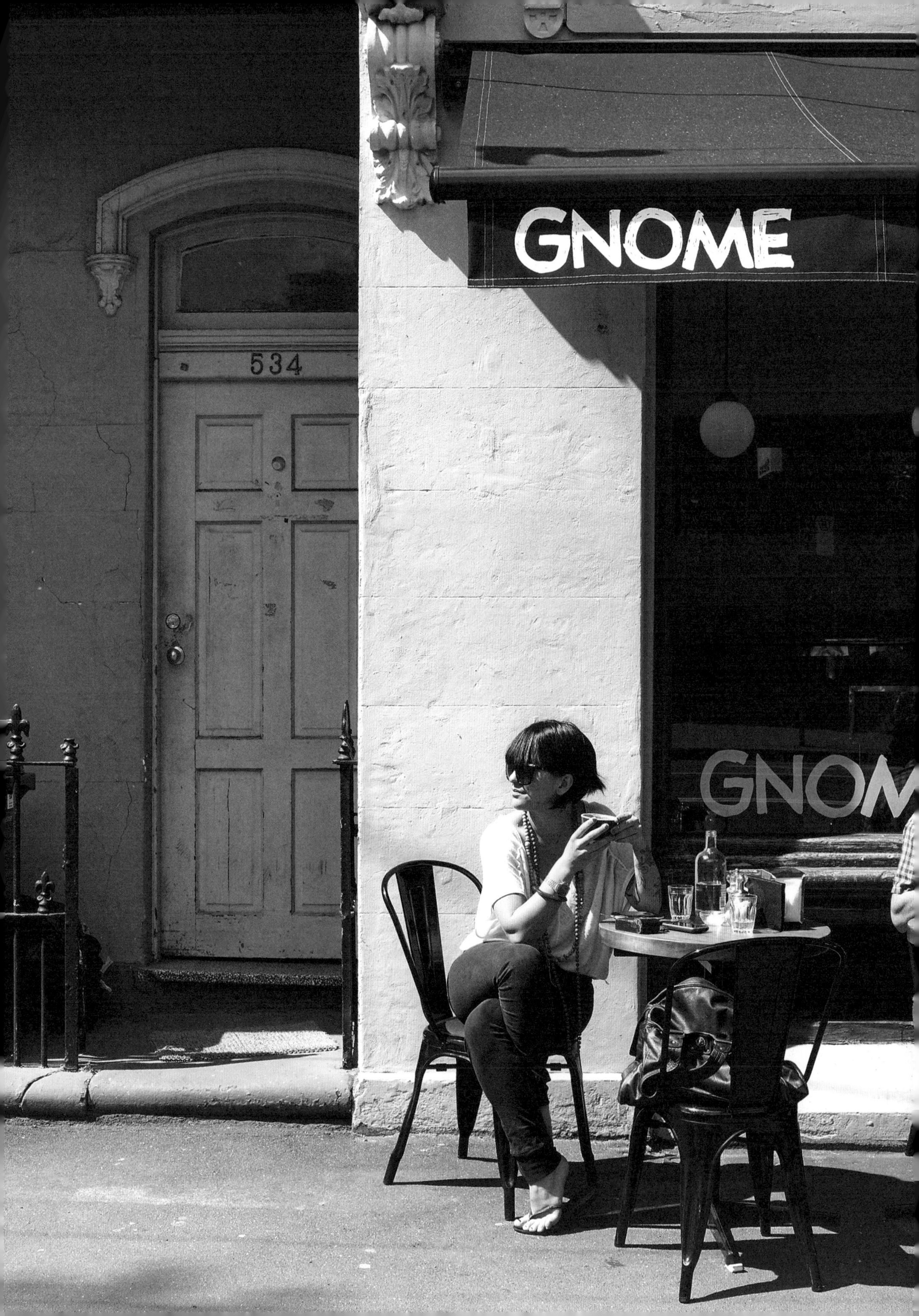
GNOME
534
GNOM

THIS IS BY FAR THE EASIEST AND QUICKEST WAY TO COOK A LEG OF LAMB. THE COOKING METHOD I USE HERE WAS INSPIRED BY A THREE-HAT RESTAURANT WHERE I ONCE WORKED. WE USED MILK-FED LAMB BECAUSE OF ITS TENDER, CREAMY TEXTURE BUT ANY LEG OF LAMB WILL DO. THE MARINADE WORKS EQUALLY WELL WITH THE MORE ROBUST FLAVOUR OF MUTTON.

BARBECUED BUTTERFLIED LAMB LEG MARINATED WITH LEMON, GARLIC & PARSLEY

4 SERVES / MAIN

1 lamb leg
grated zest and juice of 2 lemons
4 garlic cloves, finely chopped

1 bunch of parsley, finely chopped
100 ml (3½ oz) olive oil

Lay the lamb leg on a chopping board with the inside of the leg facing up. (This is the side that is flatter in appearance.) Look at the joint to see the structure of the bones. Using a sharp knife, cut down to the bone at the top of the leg. Carefully work your way along and around the bone as you gently remove the meat, working towards the bottom of the leg. You should now have one piece of boneless leg that you have managed to do yourself. If you have a dog, I'm sure they will gratefully take care of the bone for you.

Lay the leg on a chopping board, rolling the meat out flat. Try to make the depth of the meat as even as possible by splaying any thick pieces of meat open, being careful not to cut right through.

Mix the lemon zest and juice, garlic, parsley and olive oil and some salt and freshly ground black pepper together in a large bowl. Add the lamb leg and massage with the marinade, then cover and place in the fridge to marinate for 2 hours.

Heat a barbecue grill to medium–high heat. Remove the lamb from the marinade, reserving the marinade for basting. Lay the lamb on the barbecue and cook for 5 minutes. Turn it 90 degrees, baste generously with the marinade and cook for 5 minutes. Turn the lamb over, again baste with the marinade and cook for 5 minutes. Turn the lamb 90 degrees, baste again and cook for a further 5 minutes. Remove to a plate, cover with foil and allow to rest for 10 minutes. Place the lamb leg back on the barbecue for 5 minutes or so to warm through, then slice and serve.

LAMB CHUMP MINI ROASTS MARINATED WITH ROSEMARY, OLIVES & GARLIC

4 SERVES / MAIN

4 lamb chumps, trimmed of excess fat
½ bunch of rosemary, finely chopped
200 g (7 oz) kalamata olives, pitted and
  roughly chopped

2 garlic cloves, finely chopped
2 tablespoons olive oil, plus extra,
  for frying

Place the lamb chumps on a chopping board with the top of the chump facing up. (This is the side that will still have some fat over it.) Using a very sharp knife, cut a horizontal pocket about 5 mm (¼ inch) from the top of the chumps almost right through to the other side.

Place the chumps in a bowl and add the rosemary, olives, garlic and olive oil. Mix well and season with a little sea salt and freshly ground black pepper. Place in the fridge and marinate for at least 4 hours, or overnight. Remove the chumps from the bowl, scraping them clean of the marinade. Place the marinade in a food processor and process to form a coarse paste. Using a spoon, insert a generous amount of the paste into the pockets in the lamb and close the ends with toothpicks.

Preheat the oven to 160°C (315°F/Gas 2–3). Place an ovenproof frying pan on the stovetop over medium heat. Add a little olive oil, then carefully place the lamb chumps, pocket side down, in the frying pan. Cook until the surface of the meat is lightly and evenly browned, then turn the chumps over. Place the lamb in the oven and cook for 12 minutes for medium-rare, or cook to your liking. Remove the lamb from the oven and allow to rest for 5 minutes. Serve either whole or sliced.

CHARGRILLED BACKSTRAP MARINATED IN LEMON, YOGHURT & MINT

4 SERVES / MAIN

1 small onion, roughly chopped
4 garlic cloves, roughly chopped
grated zest and juice of 1 lemon
200 g (7 oz) natural Greek yoghurt

1 large handful of mint leaves, roughly
   chopped
4 x 200 g (7 oz) lamb backstraps
2½ tablespoons olive oil

Purée the onion and garlic in a food processor, then add the lemon zest, half the yoghurt and half the mint. Season the yoghurt mixture with salt and freshly ground black pepper, then add the lamb backstraps and mix well. Cover and marinate in the fridge for 2 hours.

To make a dressing, whisk the remaining yoghurt and the lemon juice together in a bowl, then slowly add the olive oil, whisking the ingredients together as you would to make mayonnaise. Stir through the remaining mint and season with salt and freshly ground black pepper. Set aside for later use.

Remove the lamb backstraps from the marinade, scraping most of the marinade from the meat, and let it sit at room temperature for 15 minutes. To cook the backstraps, heat a chargrill pan over medium–high heat, add the lamb and cook to your liking — medium-rare will be about 3–5 minutes each side. Remove the lamb from the pan and allow the meat to rest for 5 minutes before slicing. Serve with the yoghurt and mint dressing.

IF YOU HAVE YOUR OWN MINCER, YOU CAN BUY GOOD-QUALITY PIECES OF MEAT AND MINCE THEM YOURSELF. FOR THIS RECIPE, BUY WHOLE PIECES OF LAMB BREAST; WHEN MINCED, YOU'LL HAVE A PERFECT BALANCE OF MEAT TO FAT.

SPICED STICKY LAMB MINCE

4 SERVES / MAIN

500 g (1 lb 2 oz) minced (ground) lamb
2 tablespoons vegetable oil
4 red Asian shallots, finely diced
2 garlic cloves, finely chopped

2 bird's eye chillies, very finely sliced
1 teaspoon finely chopped ginger
3 tablespoons kecap manis
2 teaspoons Maggi seasoning sauce

Bring 2 litres (70 fl oz/8 cups) of water to the boil in a wok or saucepan, then add the lamb mince. Once the water returns to the boil, pour the water and lamb through a sieve placed over a bowl. Reserve the lamb for later use. Allow the fat to set on top of the water, then scoop it off and discard it in the rubbish before throwing the water away.

Wipe the wok clean and place it over medium heat. Add the oil and fry the shallots, garlic, chilli and ginger for 1–2 minutes until fragrant. Add the lamb, stir to combine, then stir-fry for a couple of minutes. Add the kecap manis and Maggi sauce and toss everything together to combine the flavours. Serve with rice.

GRILLED LAMB CHOPS MARINATED IN BEAN CURD

4 SERVES / MAIN

2 garlic cloves, finely chopped
6 spring onions (scallions), white part only, finely sliced
1 long red chilli, finely sliced
100 g (3½ oz) fermented bean curd

1 tablespoon fish sauce
1 tablespoon sugar
2 tablespoons vegetable oil
1 kg (2 lb 4 oz) lamb forequarter chops

Pound the garlic, spring onion and chilli into a paste using a mortar and pestle. Place the fermented bean curd into a bowl, add the spring onion paste, fish sauce, sugar and vegetable oil and mix together. Add the lamb chops and mix to evenly coat them with the marinade. Place in the fridge and marinate for 1 hour, or up to 4 hours.

Preheat the grill (broiler) to medium. Place the chops on the grill tray in a single layer and grill for about 3 minutes each side for medium-rare, or cook to your liking.

YOU DON'T SEE LAMB'S BRAINS ON MENUS MUCH ANYMORE AND SOME OF YOU MAY SAY THAT'S FOR A GOOD REASON. THE TRUTH IS, CRUMBED AND DEEP-FRIED LIKE THIS, THEY ARE INCREDIBLE AND VERY, VERY EDIBLE. YOU CAN CRUMB THEM TWICE FOR AN EXTRA CRUNCHY FINISH IF YOU LIKE, JUST MAKE A DOUBLE QUANTITY OF THE GREMOLATA.

GREMOLATA-CRUMBED DEEP-FRIED LAMB'S BRAINS

4 SERVES / STARTER

6 lamb's brains
milk, to cover
1 small onion, peeled
2 garlic cloves, crushed
1 bay leaf
plain (all-purpose) flour, for dusting
1 egg, lightly whisked, for coating
vegetable oil, for deep-frying

GREMOLATA
100 g (3½ oz/1¼ cups) breadcrumbs
    made from stale bread
½ bunch of parsley, finely chopped
grated zest of 1 large lemon
2 garlic cloves, finely chopped

Soak the brains overnight in heavily salted water. Remove the brains from the water, place them in a saucepan and pour in enough milk to cover. Add the onion, garlic and bay leaf to the pan and place it over medium heat. Bring the milk to the boil, then reduce the heat and simmer the brains gently for 10 minutes.

Remove the pan from the heat and allow the brains to cool in the pan to a temperature where you can comfortably handle them. Pick the brains up and split each brain in half into two lobes. Using a paring knife, carefully remove and discard any membrane that covers the outside of the brain. Place the brains on a tray and refrigerate for 30 minutes to set.

Meanwhile, to make the gremolata, combine the breadcrumbs, parsley, lemon zest and garlic in a bowl.

Remove the brains from the fridge and dust them with the flour, dip them in the egg, then roll and coat them well with the gremolata crumbs. Once all the brains are crumbed, one-third fill a large heavy-based saucepan or deep-fryer with vegetable oil and heat to 180°C (350°F), or until a cube of bread dropped into the oil turns golden brown in 15 seconds. Carefully add the brains and fry until they are golden brown. Remove and drain on paper towel, season with sea salt and serve.

BEEF

CONTENTS

& VEAL 211

BEEF

I EAT MEAT BUT IF YOU CHOOSE NOT TO I RESPECT YOUR DECISION. AS A NATION WE ARE GENERALLY OBSESSED WITH EATING BEEF AND THIS HASN'T CHANGED SINCE I WAS YOUNG. I GREW UP IN THE SUBURBS OF BRISBANE IN THE SEVENTIES AND EIGHTIES. IT WAS A TIME WHEN PEOPLE WITH AN ANGLO-CELTIC HERITAGE MADE UP APPROXIMATELY 70 PER CENT OF AUSTRALIA'S POPULATION. THE BRITISH HAVE A REPUTATION FOR ENJOYING THE PLEASURES OF THE FLESH — ESPECIALLY WHEN IT IS SLOWLY ROASTED AND SERVED WITH HOT ENGLISH MUSTARD AND YORKSHIRE PUDDING — SO MUCH SO THAT AT ONE POINT IN HISTORY THE ENGLISH TURNED IRELAND INTO ONE BIG CATTLE PASTURE TO HELP SATISFY ITS DOMESTIC BEEF DEMAND.

My mother's ancestry is Welsh. She is, and always has been, very particular about her beef. She would think nothing of driving across town to buy the family's meat supply for the week. But the quality had to be right and, it goes without saying, it had to represent good value. Back then, a butcher shop took pride of place on the main street and a good butcher was a man of high standing in the community. Customers were very loyal to their butcher and my mum was no exception. But if the meat supply went bad, and successive meals were ruined, a relationship that was forged over many years could be instantly severed. Then Mum would turn to the 'neighbourhood beef grapevine' and be off in search of another supplier.

As children we ate a lot of beef. Mum would pan-fry, roast or grill our steaks to perfection. The meat was always served with one vegetable for starch and carbohydrate and two vegetables for vitamins and fibre. In other words, we were the typical 'steak and three veg' Australian family.

Mum did all the cooking and also worked at night, so she found it was easier to manage if she kept her repertoire simple. She perfected a cyclic menu where the meals would roll over from week to week, leaving enough of a gap between like meals so it wouldn't feel too repetitive. There was one exception: Sunday night was roast dinner night, and it was our family's way to welcome in the new week.

I look back on the food we ate as children with fondness. The food wasn't lavished with exotic influence — there were no foreign ingredients, herbs or spices — but it was comforting and nourishing and, back then, everyone I knew ate that way. In fact, I would say the food we ate then was healthier (and served in better portions) than what most people eat today.

THE BEEF INDUSTRY IN AUSTRALIA

I'm reasonably familiar with farm life and working with cattle. Friends of our family own a mixed farm in southeast Queensland, an area famous for beef production. They run mostly beef cattle but also keep a small herd of dairy cattle and grow various vegetable and fodder crops. We spent many of our school holidays there, although it's probably more appropriate to describe our time there as a 'working' holiday, as more often than not we were kept

occupied with farm chores. But it wasn't all work; we did manage to find time for a few overs of cricket during the day, and when the river was flowing, which wasn't very often, we'd take time out for a swim. I have fond memories of that time; I loved the no-nonsense and physical aspects of farm life. I gained an understanding of the rhythm of country life and what the change of season brings. I still use this knowledge when I buy produce for the restaurant, even though I now live in the most densely populated city in Australia.

Today, just as when I was young, the beef industry is firmly established in Australia and is internationally recognised, but its beginnings were less than certain. When Australia was colonised it is thought that two breeds of cattle were initially introduced. The first was the prized Aberdeen Angus, a member of the Bos taurus species from Scotland, and the second was the Brahman, a member of the Bos indicus species, a breed that originated in India. Unfortunately for the fledgling colony and cattle industry, there were few, if any, experienced cattlemen among the petty criminals making the journey to Australia, and several years after they arrived, cattle numbers had dwindled considerably.

It wasn't until the early part of the nineteenth century that more Angus cattle were imported into Australia and today it is the pre-eminent cattle breed. Angus cattle thrive in cooler temperate climates, such as that in southern Australia, where the grass tends to be lush. This suits the Angus, as they don't like to walk too far for a feed. The breed is popular with farmers as they are docile and renowned for their fertility, ease of calving and their ability to put on muscle mass. The less the farmer has to handle the cattle the better. The aim is to keep them stress free so they can concentrate on eating grass, putting on weight and developing the flavoursome and tender meat for which the breed is famous. The beef on your dinner plate tonight is likely to be a cut from a member of the Bos taurus family.

The Brahman is a robust breed that performs well on less-productive pastures, making it ideal for the hot and dry conditions of northern and central Australia. Importantly, it is a fairly low maintenance breed that is used to grazing over large areas of pasture, and is somewhat disease and tick resistant. The Brahman is not renowned for its eating quality, although the flavour and texture of the beef is improved by crossbreeding it with cattle from the Bos taurus family. The Murray Grey is a great Australian example of this, as the tough resilient quality of the Brahman is retained while the eating quality is improved by the influence of the Bos taurus. Brahman cattle are predominately exported to Indonesia as part of the live cattle trade.

The Australian beef industry's international reputation is remarkable considering we produce only 2.5 per cent, or 25 million head, of the 1 billion head of cattle farmed worldwide. The export sales of live cattle and beef contribute $5 billion to the economy annually, while the domestic industry is worth approximately $6.4 billion. Of all meat consumed in Australia, beef enjoys a 35 per cent share of the market, and I, for one, have only recently begun to question the industry's sustainability and environmental credentials. I admit that in the past I have paid more attention to quality and the flavour of the meat than its environmental impact.

WHAT IS MARBLE SCORING?

Today, especially in the up-market butcher shops of our capital cities, you no longer just ask the butcher for a piece of sirloin, rump or rib eye. The focus is now on the beast's breed, provenance and marble score. It's fantastic that people are now interested in breed and provenance, but I'm not convinced the preoccupation with marble score is entirely warranted.

A marble score is an indication of the amount of intramuscular fat present in a carcass of beef. Intramuscular fat runs throughout the muscles in a similar fashion to a network of arteries and veins, and is measured on a scale between 1 and 12. A score of 12+ identifies a carcass that is exceptionally marbled. This meat appears almost white and is said to be the most flavoursome and tender. The meat from grain-fed cattle tends to have more marbling throughout than that of pasture-fed cattle. The intramuscular fat in the grain-fed cattle does tend to make it more tender, but it is not the only precursor to tenderness — stress management, general health and how the animals are hung and processed post slaughter are also contributing factors. Chefs and connoisseurs actively seek out beef with a score of 6 and above. The higher the score, the more expensive the meat, and prices of $160 a kilogram and above are not uncommon. In a restaurant you would expect to pay between $150 and $200 for a 250-gram steak.

This price may seem exorbitant but the cost of producing grain-fed beef is significantly higher than pasture-fed. To achieve a high marble score, cattle are fed grain for up to 600 days in a feedlot. Grain is expensive and the feedlot companies generally buy their grain on the open market. Although, to reduce costs, some of the larger companies have integrated the growing of grain into their business model. The quantity and quality of the grain offered on the market is directly influenced by the prevailing climatic conditions. Because of this, grain prices can be quite volatile and fluctuate significantly depending on the overall global harvest.

To pocket the maximum return on their investment, feedlot companies need cattle to convert the grain they eat into muscle mass as efficiently as possible. A feedlot presents the perfect environment for accelerating growth. The high-kilojoule diet is carefully formulated and delivered to the cattle at regular intervals throughout the day. This constant availability of food and water, and the limited exercise the cattle get within the yard, ensures the cattle bulk up quickly. Typically, beef for general consumption comes from cattle that are slaughtered at 18 months of age. The meat from these young cattle, if managed well and fed a grain diet, will be tender but it probably won't show much, or any, marbling. The British breeds found in feedlots — Hereford, Angus and Shorthorn — need to live to at least 24 months to lay down any significant intramuscular fat. However, there is a breed of cattle that does marble well feeding exclusively on fodder crops; this is the Japanese breed we know collectively as Wagyu. Wagyu cattle are renowned for their ability to marble. When these animals are fed grain (up to a maximum of 550 days in feedlots), their meat is a mass of fine white lines of fat.

I use Gundooee certified organic Wagyu beef at Red Lantern. Being certified organic, this beef is free of antibiotics and growth hormones and although the cattle can be fed organically grown grain, the beef I use has only ever grazed on pasture. It takes 36 months of slow and patient growing before these cattle are ready to be sent to slaughter. The beef isn't highly marbled when compared to grain-fed Wagyu but the flavour and mouthfeel is delicious and unique.

I THINK IT'S IMPORTANT FOR CITY KIDS TO EXPERIENCE LIFE ON A FARM, IF ONLY TO GAIN AN APPRECIATION OF THE FOOD PRODUCTION CYCLE. UNDERSTANDING WHERE THEIR FOOD COMES FROM MAY ENCOURAGE THEM TO SEEK OUT AND APPRECIATE WHOLESOME FOOD, INSTEAD OF THE CONVENIENT AND SHORT-LIVED FIX OF FAST FOOD. WHO KNOWS, THE EXPERIENCE MAY EVEN ENTICE THEM TO WANT TO COOK.

GRAIN-FED OR PASTURE-FED BEEF?

I have eaten my fair share of grain-fed beef throughout my career and I'll admit most of it I have thoroughly enjoyed. When I started out in the restaurant industry 15 years ago, chefs and restaurant customers expected their beef to be grain-fed — it was perceived to be more consistently tender than its pasture-fed counterpart. Yes, grain-fed beef was generally more consistent, but today, with improved genetic identification, animal husbandry and farming practice, this isn't exclusively true.

Nowadays I'll occasionally eat a grain-fed steak, especially if it is dry-aged, sliced thickly and chargrilled rare over a wood-fired grill, but 99 per cent of all the beef I eat is pasture-fed. I prefer to eat pasture-fed beef as I find its taste and texture more enjoyable. I like knowing the cattle that produce the beef I eat have enjoyed a good quality of life, only available on the open range. Refreshingly, 75 per cent of all cattle in Australia are reared in this way. Happy, healthy cattle equal happy, healthy people. It is now known that the meat from pasture-fed cattle is better for you: it contains higher levels of vitamins and Omega-3 fatty acids and much lower levels of Omega-6 fatty acids than its grain-fed counterpart. Grains and cereals contain high levels of Omega-6; if we eat the meat of cattle that have themselves consumed large amounts of grain, it only adds to our intake of Omega-6. By feeding cattle grain, we have changed the natural balance of fatty acid present in the meat of our livestock.

Today a greater number of people are taking an interest in how their food is produced, and are expressing a preference for pasture-fed beef. They believe, as I do, that cattle should be free to graze on pasture and not be fed grain, especially not in feedlots. Cows are ruminant animals; their digestive system is fundamentally designed to digest grass. In fact, when they first enter a feedlot their diet has to be carefully prescribed. Before the grain and cereals can become the mainstay of their diet, it is fed to them in small doses mixed with silage, such as hay. The ratio of grain and cereal to silage is gradually increased until the animal's stomach microorganisms accept and can actually digest the grain. If this is not done properly a condition called acidosis can occur.

Although some cattle are fed for up to 300 days in feedlots, typically the beef on the supermarket shelf is from cattle that have been fed for 90 to 120 days. (It is interesting to note that cattle can be fed grain for up to 60 days and still be sold as grass-fed.) Cattle in feedlots consume about 20 kilograms of grain per day and with every 9 kilograms of grain they eat, they gain 1 kilogram of body mass; this is known as the food conversion ratio. As you can see, the overwhelming majority of grain is eaten just to keep the animal alive.

We now live in a world with questionable future food security. International stockpiles of grains and cereals are on the decline. Many people believe the grain currently used to feed cattle could be used to feed the millions of hungry people in the world. This argument is based on the aforementioned food conversion ratio — you can feed more people with the grain currently used to feed cattle than you can with the beef produced from the cattle that have eaten the grain.

Environmentalists question the sustainability of the industry because of its inefficient use of natural resources. Grain needs to be cultivated, harvested and then transported to the feedlots. This in itself requires a substantial amount of water, but the cattle themselves also need to drink water to survive. There are figures available that show the amount of water used to produce every 1 kilogram of beef, but these figures range from quite insignificant to extreme, depending on the formula you use. Another environmental consideration is the amount of greenhouse gas the cattle generate while digesting their food. I had assumed the majority of methane gas emitted by cattle was a result of them farting. Well, I was wrong. Most of the gas is produced when the cattle regurgitate or burp up grain or grass from their stomachs to 'chew the cud'. Methane gas is known to be twenty times more damaging to the ozone than carbon dioxide.

Animal activists voice their concerns for the welfare of cattle in feedlots. It may, or may not, surprise you to know that animal welfare is important to the operator of the feedlot as well — although their concern is possibly motivated by the fact that a stress-free healthy animal is an efficient food-converting animal.

Regulations exist for the design and construction of feedlots, and there are rules specifying how the animals are to be treated within the system. The amount of room each animal has to move around, access to food and water, and shelter from the elements are all considered. I believe, even though regulations exist, there is no substitute for the open range, especially when shelter is provided for inclement weather. The majority of feedlots in Australia are operated to best practice standards. Whether the existing standards are satisfactory is debatable.

To its credit, the beef industry, unlike some others, is refreshingly open. Whether you agree with how the operators conduct their businesses or not, they are quite open to public scrutiny. I wanted to see a feedlot operation for myself. OK, I'll admit my host possibly strategically selected the feedlot. It was a medium-sized operation in western NSW and on the day of my visit it was running at two-thirds capacity. What really surprised me about the cattle, and on reflection maybe it shouldn't have, was how healthy they looked. They weren't as clean as pasture-raised cattle, their bellies were dirty with a mixture of mud and excrement, but they showed no sign of being ill or mistreated. While I prefer to eat grass-fed beef for my own ethical (and culinary) reasons, I try to keep an open mind.

GROWTH HORMONES AND ANTIBIOTICS

The mere mention of these two words in a discussion on food production is enough to polarise a room. Unlike the chicken industry where growth hormones are not used, the Australian beef industry does use Hormonal Growth Promotants (HGPs) to accelerate cattle growth. The hormones are implanted into the cow's ear, and the hormone is slowly released over time. The World Health Organization (WHO) has scientifically proven that meat from cattle implanted with natural HGPs is safe to eat. Apparently you would have to eat, '77 kilograms of beef in one sitting to ingest the same amount of oestrogen that is found in one egg'. Growth promotants are banned in the European Union but WHO found that the ban was not supported by science.

HGPs have been found to increase growth in cattle by 10–30 per cent, and better the food conversion ratio by as much as 15 per cent. Because of these statistics, some people believe hormones have the potential to create a better outcome for the environment. By using the hormones, farmers can run fewer cattle and still manage to satisfy our demand for beef – and the cattle eat a lot less grain or grass in the process.

Antibiotics are used in the cattle industry to treat sick animals, although there seems to be little conclusive evidence to suggest the antibiotics are detrimental to our health. That said, WHO has recommended the use of individual prescriptions to treat sick animals and

Aged Pasture Fed
Rolled Scotch Fillet
Roast $46.99
p/kg

Aged pasture fed
rolled sirloin roast
$46.99 p/kg

Kurobuta Pork
Loin Roast $34.99
p/kg

Dry aged pasture
fed rump steaks
$58.99 p/kg

Aged pasture fed
scotch fillet $46.99 p/kg

not have antibiotics administered to all the animals within an intensive farming system. At the feedlot I visited, any unwell animals were taken to a 'hospital yard' where their condition was assessed and drugs were administered, if necessary. The greatest fear with prescribing antibiotics to animals within our food system is that we may be inadvertently creating super viruses and viruses that can be transmitted from animal to human.

If the issue of hormone and antibiotic use is truly a concern for you, I suggest you do as I do and buy organic beef. Organic beef is independently audited and is certified to be free of hormones and antibiotics.

TOWARDS A SUSTAINABLE FUTURE

I feel the feedlot industry is listening to some of our concerns and is making an effort to address both the environmental and animal welfare issues. They recognise we want better outcomes for the environment and for the animals. It is hoped that by improving the food conversion ratio (getting the cattle to consume less while gaining more weight) and reducing the overall water usage, the beef industry can improve its environmental footprint. By collecting data and identifying the animals that are more efficient at converting food into muscle mass, better performing animals can be selectively bred. To date, the work done by the Australian cattle industry has led to the overall cattle herd being smaller today than it was 20 years ago, but it is managing to produce more beef.

It has been suggested that if we were truly serious about combating climate change we would give up beef altogether. We could all eat a little less meat and include more fruit and vegetables in our diet, but perhaps by opting to eat pasture-fed beef we are in fact doing our thing for the environment. Scientist Tim Flannery has stated that pasture-fed beef is environmentally sustainable because cattle are moved regularly from one paddock to another. It's a perfect cycle: the cows eat the grass, digest it and excrete it, then the manure fertilises the soil and the grass is given time to grow again. This is how my friend Rob Lennon raises his organic Wagyu and why I choose to use his beef in my restaurant.

Cattle producers are changing the way they do business. Change is not always easy, as it requires a certain leap of faith — a leap into the unknown is sometimes loaded with uncertainty. To my delight I've found the Australian beef industry is, for the greater part, embracing change and adopting sustainable farming practices. It is often said that farmers are the caretakers of the land; their very livelihood depends on a healthy environment. They now know all too well the ill effects of bad land management. You don't need to gaze into a crystal ball to see what will happen to the beef industry if it doesn't strive for more sustainable farming practice.

There is a growing appreciation in Australia and around the world of the importance of harmonious ecosystems and the need for sustainable farming methods. It appears we may be going 'back to the future' where science and traditional farming methods combine to achieve this goal.

VEAL

IN KEEPING WITH MY OVERALL FOOD PHILOSOPHY, 'EAT EVERYTHING, WASTE NOTHING', IF YOU DRINK MILK AND EAT BEEF, THEN YOU SHOULD EAT VEAL AS WELL. BUT WHY DOES ONE LEAD TO THE OTHER?

Vealers (calves grown specifically for veal) are a part of the natural rhythm of life on a dairy farm. Dairy cows are impregnated annually so they can produce and provide milk throughout the year. About half the calves born will be female, and most of these will be raised to replace or sustain the dairy herd numbers. The male calves, however, don't serve any purpose on a dairy farm, so are sold to farmers who raise them for their meat. They will live a very short life, on average 6 months.

Physically, dairy cattle are quite different to beef cattle. They don't 'fill out' as beef cattle do and if you look at the two breeds side by side you would think the dairy cow was considerably underfed. Dairy cattle don't convert food into muscle mass efficiently like the beef breeds, and this inability confines the male calves to their destiny.

Initially, vealers are fed a concentrated milk formula high in colostrum, which gives them the essential vitamins and minerals for healthy growth. Roughage is introduced to the diet after a day or so, although the calves will continue to drink milk or milk concentrate throughout their lives. The calves' diet should contain sufficient iron to prevent them from becoming anaemic, but in some parts of the world this is not always the case.

Most of the criticism of the industry stems from the fact that in parts of Europe and in North America the desired colour for veal is white. To achieve this, the calves are fed a diet severely lacking in iron and are confined to indoor stalls — a cruel practice where their necks are tied to severely restrict movement — to promote the soft milky texture of the flesh. The muscles are so weakened by the lack of use that the animals are barely able to stand. These unfortunate calves endure so much unnecessary suffering in their short lives. In addition, stress and a predominately milk diet can cause diarrhoea and breathing problems. Fortunately this method of veal production is receiving the condemnation it deserves and is gradually being banned.

In Australia, calves are either raised on open pasture or in climate-controlled sheds where they live in small groups in pens and interact freely with each other. All calves within the Australian veal industry enjoy a diet that fulfils their recommended daily iron requirement, they are fed fresh milk or a milk substitute and are either grass- or grain-fed. Vealers raised on open pasture are by far the luckier of the two, although the conditions for the intensively raised calves aren't as grim as those experienced by beef cattle in feedlots.

The two main seasons for veal are spring and autumn. This naturally coincides with the gestation periods of the dairy cattle. When it comes to buying veal, the meat should be pink or have reddish hues and the fat should be white. The colour in Australian veal comes from the iron in the calves' diet. Veal that was fed fresh milk always cooks better than veal that was fed milk substitute, because it retains much of its moisture as it cooks. Ask your butcher if the veal was fed fresh milk and also if it was pasture-fed.

SWEET & SPICY BEEF MEATBALLS

4 SERVES / MAIN

2½ tablespoons olive oil
500 g (1 lb 2 oz) onions, finely sliced
3 garlic cloves, finely chopped
1 kg (2 lb 4 oz) minced (ground) beef
½ bunch of parsley, finely chopped
½ bunch of coriander (cilantro), finely
   chopped
1 teaspoon ground cumin

½ teaspoon ground ginger
1 teaspoon ground allspice
2 teaspoons smoked paprika
2 teaspoons salt
1 egg
olive oil, for frying
2 quantities tomato sauce (page 32)
shaved parmesan cheese, to serve

Place a large deep-sided frying pan over medium heat. Add the olive oil, onion and garlic to the pan and gently cook, stirring occasionally, for 15–20 minutes, or until the onions are nicely caramelised. Pour them into a large bowl and allow to cool completely.

Add the beef, herbs, spices, salt and egg to the bowl and mix well to combine. Lightly wet your hands with water and roll the mince mixture into balls. You can shape the mince into 8 large balls roughly the size of a tennis ball, or into 25–30 smaller balls.

Pan-fry the meatballs in batches in a large frying pan over medium heat for 15–20 minutes (or 10–12 minutes for the smaller ones), or until just cooked through, turning them in the pan occasionally. Alternatively, you can brush the meatballs with some olive oil, place them on greased baking trays and roast in a 200°C (400°F/Gas 6) oven for 20–25 minutes for the larger meatballs or 15 minutes for the smaller ones.

Reheat the tomato sauce and serve with the meatballs. Garnish with the shaved parmesan and season with freshly ground black pepper.

VIETNAMESE BRAISED BLADE STEAK WITH GREEN PEPPERCORNS

4-6 SERVES / MAIN

1 kg (2 lb 4 oz) piece of bolar blade
3 tablespoons fish sauce
2 tablespoons dark soy sauce
2½ tablespoons peanut oil
100 g (3½ oz) red Asian shallots, finely chopped
1 tablespoon finely chopped garlic
2 tablespoons caster (superfine) sugar

3 lemongrass stalks, white part only, finely sliced
2 litres (70 fl oz/8 cups) chicken stock or water
3 tablespoons green peppercorns
4 kaffir lime (makrut) leaves, very finely sliced

Place the blade on a clean chopping board and slice across the grain to form 2 cm (¾ inch) wide steaks. Lay the steaks out on the board and cut into 2 cm (¾ inch) wide strips, then cut these strips into 4 cm (1½ inch) long pieces. Place the beef in a bowl and marinate with the combined fish sauce and soy sauce for 30 minutes.

Heat half the peanut oil in a wok. Remove the beef from the marinade, reserving the marinade. Add the beef to the wok in batches and seal over high heat. Once all the beef is browned, tip it into a bowl. Wipe the wok clean with paper towel, then place the wok over low heat and add the remaining oil. Add the shallots, garlic and sugar and fry very gently for 5 minutes, then increase the heat and add the lemongrass.

Return the beef to the wok, with the reserved marinade and the cooking juices. Stir well to combine the flavours, then add the stock or water. Bring the beef quickly to the boil and skim off any impurities that rise to the surface. Half cover the wok with a lid, then reduce the heat to a slow simmer and cook for 45 minutes, stirring occasionally. Remove the lid and add the green peppercorns and lime leaves, then increase the heat slightly and cook for another 30 minutes, or until the beef is very tender. The sauce should be reduced by about two-thirds. Season to taste and serve.

THERE ARE ACTUALLY TWO PARTS TO A PIECE OF BEEF BLADE AND BOTH CUTS ARE REASONABLY INEXPENSIVE. THE OYSTER BLADE IS THE PREMIUM CUT AND IS IDEAL FOR GRILLING AND STIR-FRYING WHEREAS THE BOLAR BLADE IS PERFECT FOR ROASTING OR BRAISING.

BEEF CHEEKS BRAISED IN BEER WITH AROMATIC SPICES

4-6 SERVES / MAIN

3 star anise
1 cinnamon stick
4 cloves
2 teaspoons black peppercorns
1 teaspoon Chinese five-spice
100 ml (3½ fl oz) fish sauce
1 tablespoon dark soy sauce
2 tablespoons grated palm sugar (jaggery)

350 ml (12 fl oz) beer (I like to use
   Vietnamese 333 beer)
1 kg (2 lb 4 oz) trimmed beef cheeks
2 tablespoons vegetable oil
1 onion, diced
3 garlic cloves, finely chopped
2 litres (70 fl oz/8 cups) beef stock
coriander (cilantro) sprigs, to garnish
sliced long red chilli, to garnish

Gently fry the star anise, cinnamon, cloves and black peppercorns in a dry frying pan until fragrant. Allow the spices to cool, then grind them into a fine powder using a mortar and pestle. Mix the ground spices and five-spice in a large bowl, then add the fish sauce, dark soy sauce, palm sugar and beer, and mix well. Clean any excess fat from the beef cheeks and place them into the bowl with the spice marinade. Work the marinade into the beef cheeks, cover and place in the fridge to marinate for 2 hours.

Remove the beef cheeks from the marinade and pat dry with paper towel. Reserve the marinade for later use. Heat 1 tablespoon of the oil in a large wok or frying pan over medium heat, add the beef cheeks and seal on all sides. Remove from the wok and set aside. Wipe the wok clean with paper towel. If you aren't using a wok, you may now need to use a large pot to accommodate the rest of the ingredients. Add the remaining oil to your wok or pot and gently fry the onion for 4 minutes until soft and translucent, then add the garlic and cook for 2 minutes. Return the beef cheeks to the wok, stir to combine with the onion and garlic, then add the reserved marinade and the stock. Bring the stock to the boil and skim off any impurities that rise to the surface. Reduce the heat and simmer for 1½ hours, or until the cheeks are very tender. You may need to add extra water as the cheeks need to be covered in liquid while they cook. To check if they are cooked, pass a skewer through the middle of the meat; it should pass easily in and out.

Remove the cheeks from the wok and set aside. Increase the heat and reduce the liquid in the wok by half. Taste the stock as you reduce it; if you reduce it too far the flavour will become salty and too intense. To serve, slice the meat into 2.5 cm (1 inch) square pieces, then place them back into the sauce to heat through. Check the seasoning and add salt if required. Garnish with the coriander and chilli, and serve with steamed vegetables and jasmine rice.

I BELIEVE THE ULTIMATE RESPECT WE CAN SHOW AN ANIMAL RAISED FOR THE DINNER TABLE IS TO ENSURE WE CONSUME EVERYTHING FROM HEAD TO TAIL. BEEF CHEEKS ARE VERY TOUGH BECAUSE OF ALL THE WORK THEY DO, BUT WHEN COOKED SLOWLY THE MEAT PRACTICALLY DISSOLVES ON YOUR TONGUE.

I PREFER TO EAT GRASS-FED BEEF AS I BELIEVE IT HAS MORE FLAVOUR, IT'S BETTER FOR YOU AND, JUST AS IMPORTANTLY, THE COWS HAVE BEEN FREE TO GRAZE ON PASTURE.

SLOW-ROASTED BEEF FILLET WITH BORDELAISE SAUCE

4 SERVES / MAIN

½ bunch of thyme
2 bay leaves
finely grated zest and juice of ½ orange
2 garlic cloves, crushed
100 ml (3½ fl oz) olive oil
freshly cracked white pepper
800 g (1 lb 12 oz) beef fillet (centre cut), trimmed
500 g (1 lb 2 oz) rock salt
50 g (1¾ oz) butter

BORDELAISE SAUCE

200 g (7 oz) bone marrow (this is the marrow removed from bone — ask your butcher to remove the marrow for you)
2 tablespoons salt
200 ml (7 fl oz) good-quality red wine
8 thyme sprigs
1 bay leaf
4 spring onions (scallions), white part only, thinly sliced
6 white peppercorns
300 ml (10½ fl oz) veal stock
20 g (¾ oz) unsalted butter
1 tablespoon chopped parsley

Place the thyme, bay leaves, orange zest and juice, garlic and olive oil in a saucepan and heat gently until it starts to simmer. Remove the pan from the heat, season with sea salt and cracked white pepper and allow to cool. Clean any sinew from the fillet, place in a bowl and then pour over the marinade. Place in the fridge to marinate overnight.

Preheat the oven to 90°C (195°F/Gas ¼). Remove the fillet from the marinade and wrap it up tightly in foil (reserve the marinade for later). Place the rock salt in a roasting tin, then place the beef on top. Cook on the middle rack of the oven for 3 hours. If you have a meat thermometer, check the internal temperature: medium-rare, 50–58°C (122–136°F) or medium, 60–63°C (140–145°F). Allow the fillet to rest in a warm place for at least 10 minutes. (This step can be completed up to an hour in advance, then finished in the pan when required.)

While the beef is cooking, make the bordelaise sauce. Slice the bone marrow into 5 mm (¼ inch) thick circles. Soak in 500 ml (17 fl oz/2 cups) of water with the salt for 2 hours. Place the wine in a saucepan with the thyme, bay leaf, spring onion and peppercorns and reduce by half. Add the stock and simmer gently until the sauce has thickened slightly and coats the back of a spoon. Strain into a clean saucepan, discarding the herbs, spring onion and peppercorns. Place the bone marrow in a saucepan of cold water and bring to the boil. Once the water boils, remove the marrow immediately. Meanwhile, reheat the sauce and whisk in the butter. Add the bone marrow and parsley to the sauce and check the seasoning.

When the beef has rested, remove the foil and cut the fillet into four portions. Place a frying pan over medium heat and add the butter and 2 tablespoons of the reserved marinade. Brown the beef on all sides while constantly basting with the butter. Place the beef on individual plates and spoon the bordelaise sauce over the top.

PAN-FRIED RIB EYE CUTLETS WITH SAGE & ANCHOVY BUTTER

4 SERVES / MAIN

4 rib eye cutlets
3 tablespoons fish sauce
2½ tablespoons olive oil
100 g (3½ oz) unsalted butter

2 garlic cloves, crushed
6 anchovy fillets
½ bunch of sage, leaves picked

Preheat the oven to 170°C (325°F/Gas 3). Scrape the bone of the eye cutlets with a boning or short non-flexible knife to clean and remove any meat or sinew, then wrap the bones tightly with foil to protect them during cooking. Lay the cutlets on a plate and drizzle the fish sauce evenly over both sides, then season with freshly ground black pepper.

Place a large ovenproof frying pan over medium–high heat, then add half the olive oil. When the oil is hot, place the cutlets in the pan and seal on one side for about 2 minutes, or until the surface of the meat is lightly golden brown, then turn the cutlets over. Place the pan and the cutlets in the oven and cook for a further 8 minutes for medium-rare, or cook to your liking. In time and with practice it will be possible to cook your cutlets to the precise degree of doneness. Remove the cutlets from the oven and place them on a tray to rest, bone side down, for half of the total cooking time. Pour off any fat that has gathered in the pan.

Place the frying pan over low heat and add the butter, garlic and anchovies. When the butter has melted, add the remaining olive oil and increase the heat slightly. Add the sage leaves and stir constantly until the sage starts to fry. Return the cutlets to the pan to warm through and baste with the sage and anchovy butter. Place a cutlet on each serving plate. Taste the sauce for seasoning and adjust if necessary, then spoon the sauce over the cutlets.

DICED SKIRT STEAK WOK-TOSSED WITH OYSTER SAUCE

4 SERVES / MAIN

3 tablespoons oyster sauce
2 teaspoons light soy sauce
2 teaspoons fish sauce
½ teaspoon white pepper
½ teaspoon caster (superfine) sugar
1 teaspoon sesame oil
800 g (1 lb 12 oz) skirt steak

1 tablespoon vegetable oil
1 small onion, cut into thin wedges
2 garlic cloves, finely chopped
1 teaspoon finely chopped ginger
1 teaspoon toasted sesame seeds,
   for garnish

Mix the oyster sauce, soy sauce and fish sauce together in a small bowl, then stir through the white pepper, sugar and sesame oil. Set the sauce aside.

Remove all the silver skin from the skirt steak, then cut the steak into 2 cm (¾ inch) cubes. Heat a wok over very high heat. Working quickly, add 1 teaspoon of the vegetable oil to the wok and a third of the meat. Fry the beef, stirring occasionally, for 2 minutes, then tip the beef into a bowl and repeat the process with the remaining beef. Once all the beef is cooked, wipe the wok clean with paper towel.

Return the wok to the heat and add the remaining teaspoon of oil, the onion, garlic and ginger. Stirring constantly, fry the ingredients for 30 seconds, then add all the beef. Toss and stir the beef to distribute it evenly in the wok. Add the sauce and wok-toss the beef with the sauce for 1 minute. Transfer the beef mixture to a serving plate and garnish with the sesame seeds.

HOW I LIKE TO MARINATE RUMP STEAK FOR THE BARBECUE

4 SERVES / MAIN

2 tablespoons kecap manis
1 tablespoon fish sauce
1 garlic clove, finely diced

1 teaspoon minced pickled red chilli
1 tablespoon olive oil
4 x 300 g (10 ½ oz) rump steaks

To make the marinade, combine the kecap manis, fish sauce, garlic, pickled chilli and olive oil in a bowl, then spread it evenly over both sides of the steaks. This is an instant marinade but you can leave the meat to marinate for longer if you like.

Heat a lightly oiled barbecue to medium–high. Cook the steaks for 3 minutes each side for medium-rare, or until cooked to your liking. Rest for 3 minutes before serving.

CHARGRILLED SIRLOIN WITH A MUSTARD & HERB CRUST

4 SERVES / MAIN

50 g (1¾ oz) unsalted butter, softened
1 tablespoon wholegrain mustard
1 teaspoon English mustard (optional)
2 tablespoons finely chopped mixed herbs,
    such as oregano, parsley and thyme

100 g (3½ oz/1¼ cups) coarse fresh
    breadcrumbs
4 x 250 g (9 oz) sirloin steaks, fat heavily
    trimmed
2 teaspoons olive oil

In a bowl, mix the butter, wholegrain mustard, English mustard (if using), chopped herbs and breadcrumbs. Season with sea salt and freshly ground black pepper and set aside.

Place a chargrill pan over medium–high heat until the pan is nice and hot. Rub the sirloin steaks with the olive oil and cook for 3 minutes, then turn the steaks over and cook the other side for 3 minutes for medium-rare. It is important to only turn the meat once. Remove the steaks from the pan and rest them on their side (narrow side down) for half the cooking time.

Preheat the grill (broiler) to high. Transfer the steaks to a grill tray and spread a generous amount of the herb and breadcrumb mixture over the steaks. Place under the grill and cook until the crust is golden brown and slightly crisp. Serve immediately.

WHETHER YOU LIKE YOUR BEEF GRAIN-
FED OR PASTURE-FED, THERE ARE THREE
MAIN CUTS USED FOR GRILLING OR ON
THE BARBECUE: SIRLOIN, RUMP AND
RIB EYE. YOUR FAVOURITE CUT MIGHT
BE DIFFERENT FROM MINE, BUT THAT'S
THE THING WITH STEAK: IT'S ALL ABOUT
PERSONAL PREFERENCE.

PRIMARY AND SECONDARY BEEF CUTS

BEEF SELLS PARTICULARLY WELL ON A MENU AND HAS A BROAD APPEAL — IT CAN BE PREPARED IN A VARIETY OF WAYS AND THERE IS A COOKING METHOD TO SUIT ALL CUTS. UNFORTUNATELY THE PRIMARY CUTS (T-BONE, RIB EYE, SIRLOIN, RUMP AND FILLET) ARE STILL THE MOST POPULAR, AS THESE ARE THE EASIEST FOR THE HOME COOK TO PREPARE. THE MEAT GENERALLY ONLY NEEDS TO BE GRILLED OR ROASTED THEN FINISHED WITH A LITTLE SALT AND PEPPER, OLIVE OIL AND MAYBE A SQUEEZE OF LEMON JUICE. BUT WHAT HAPPENS TO THE REST OF THE BEAST? THIS CREATES A PROBLEM FOR THE CATTLE PRODUCER, MEAT PROCESSOR, BUTCHER, CHEF AND, ULTIMATELY, YOU, THE CONSUMER.

Have you ever wondered why an eye fillet or rib eye roast is so expensive? Its popularity is the main reason, because it is practically guaranteed to be tender and is easy to prepare. Another less-understood reason is that primary cuts subsidise the losses made on the secondary cuts and the offal. Secondary cuts include brisket, blade, cheek, tail and chuck. Unfortunately, it is extremely difficult for processors to sell secondary cuts and offal in Australia and they generally have to seek markets offshore. The industry has to be commended for seeking out export markets and trying to educate people on just how to use these cuts.

Secondary cuts are easier to prepare than most people realise. The next time you are shopping for beef, choose a less-than-familiar cut, cook it slowly, and enjoy the yielding tenderness and richness of flavour.

THIS IS A CLASSIC FRENCH DISH AND THIS IS THE WAY I LOVE TO
COOK IT. IT'S A RECIPE THAT LETS THE INGREDIENTS SHINE AND
IT'S NOT DIFFICULT TO MAKE. I USE PASTURE-FED CHUCK STEAK
BECAUSE I FIND IT HAS THE RIGHT BALANCE OF MEAT, FAT AND
CONNECTIVE TISSUE. ANOTHER TIP IS TO USE A GOOD-QUALITY RED
WINE, ONE WITH BIG FRUIT FLAVOURS (I LIKE TO USE SHIRAZ).

BEEF BOURGUIGNON

10–12 SERVES / MAIN (FREEZE ANY LEFTOVERS FOR A LAZY DAY)

2.5 kg (5 lb 8 oz) chuck steak, cut into
   3 cm (1¼ inch) cubes
2 onions, cut into 1 cm (½ inch) dice
2 carrots, cut into 1 cm (½ inch) dice
4 garlic cloves, peeled and lightly crushed
   with the side of a knife
500 ml (17 fl oz/2 cups) red wine (I like
   to use shiraz)

2 tablespoons olive oil or beef dripping
1 tablespoon cornflour (cornstarch)
1 litre (35 fl oz/4 cups) veal stock
1 bouquet garni (a few sprigs of thyme,
   parsley and a couple of bay leaves)
chopped parsley, for garnish

Put the beef in a large bowl with the onion, carrot, garlic and wine, and stir to combine.
Cover and marinate in the fridge for 2–3 hours. Strain the beef and vegetables from the wine,
reserving the wine for later use. Separate the beef from the vegetables.

Place a casserole dish or deep frying pan over medium heat and add the olive oil or
dripping. When the oil is hot, seal the beef in small batches until well browned. Remove the
beef from the dish and set aside. Add the onion, carrot and garlic to the dish and cook for
about 10 minutes, or until soft and lightly coloured. Return the beef to the dish with the
cornflour, then stir to combine the ingredients. Add the reserved wine and simmer for
5 minutes, then add the stock and bring to the boil, skimming off any impurities that rise
to the surface. Add the bouquet garni, then reduce the heat, cover and simmer very gently
for 2 hours. Check to see if the beef is tender; if not, continue to cook until it is.

To serve, remove the bouquet garni and season with sea salt and freshly ground black
pepper. Garnish with the parsley.

YOU NEED A SERIOUSLY BIG AND THICK-CUT PIECE OF BEEF FOR THIS RECIPE. MARBLING, OR INTRAMUSCULAR FAT, IS GENERALLY AN INDICATOR OF THE TENDERNESS OF A PIECE OF BEEF AND IS TYPICALLY FOUND IN CATTLE THAT ARE FED HIGH-ENERGY GRAINS IN FEEDLOTS, ALTHOUGH IT IS POSSIBLE TO FIND MARBLING IN GRASS-FED CATTLE. ASK YOUR BUTCHER FOR GRASS-FED BEEF WITH THE HIGHEST MARBLE SCORE THEY HAVE.

BISTECCA ALLA FIORENTINA

2-4 SERVES / MAIN

1 x 1–1.5 kg (2 lb 4 oz–3 lb 5 oz) T-bone
   steak, cut 5–6 cm (2–2½ inches) thick
very good Tuscan virgin olive oil

2 bushy rosemary sprigs, tied together
   at the stem with string
juice of 1 lemon

Remove the steak from the fridge and leave at room temperature for at least 30 minutes before cooking. Pour 100 ml (3½ fl oz) of the olive oil into a bowl. Bash the rosemary with a meat mallet or the back of a knife and place it in the oil.

Preheat a chargrill pan or, for the best result, a wood-fired barbecue. Season the T-bone liberally with sea salt and freshly ground black pepper. Place the T-bone over medium heat and cook for 5 minutes. Turn the steak 90 degrees to make a crisscross pattern on the meat, then cook for a further 5 minutes. Turn the steak over and repeat the cooking process. The steak will take at least 20 minutes to reach medium-rare. If you have a meat thermometer, check the internal temperature: medium-rare, 50–58°C (122–136°F) or medium, 60–63°C (140–145°F).

Remove the steak from the pan and rest it, standing it on the T of the bone for 10 minutes. To serve, brush the meat with the olive oil using the rosemary sprigs as a brush, then place the steak back in the chargrill pan. Baste the beef occasionally with the oil while it is being warmed through. Place the T-bone on a chopping board and remove the meat from the bone. Slice the meat across the grain, then lightly rub the lemon juice and a little virgin olive oil into the meat. This will serve 4 lightweights or 2 beef connoisseurs.

FOR ME, BRISKET IS THE ULTIMATE BRAISING CUT. SURE, TRIM
OFF SOME OF THE FAT BUT LEAVE A GENEROUS AMOUNT INTACT.
BRAISING THE BRISKET WITH A LAYER OF FAT ATTACHED TO THE
MEAT REALLY MAKES THIS DISH SPECIAL.

SLOW-COOKED POINT END BRISKET WITH AROMATIC SPICES

10–12 SERVES / MAIN (FREEZE ANY LEFTOVERS FOR A LAZY DAY)

2.5 kg (5 lb 8 oz) point end beef brisket
100 ml (3½ fl oz) fish sauce
100 ml (3½ fl oz) olive oil
500 g (1 lb 2 oz) onions, finely sliced
2 tablespoons finely chopped garlic
2 tablespoons tomato paste (concentrated
   purée)
1 tablespoon ground ginger

1 tablespoon ground allspice
2 teaspoons ground cumin
3 cinnamon sticks
2 litres (70 fl oz/8 cups) chicken stock
2 x 410 g (14 oz) tins diced tomatoes
juice of 1 lemon
1 handful of coriander (cilantro) leaves

Place the brisket on a chopping board and remove any excess fat. Do not remove all of the
fat from the meat, as the fat enhances the eating experience. Cut the brisket into rectangles,
about 4 x 2 cm (1½ x ¾ inch). Place in a bowl and marinate with the fish sauce for 30 minutes.

Meanwhile, place a large heavy-based saucepan or flameproof casserole dish over medium
heat. Add the oil and, when hot, add the onions and garlic, stirring well. Reduce the heat
slightly and cook the onions, stirring occasionally, until lightly caramelised.

Increase the heat to high and add the brisket to the pan, a little at a time, and cook until
the meat is lightly browned on all sides. Add the tomato paste and stir well. Stir through all
the spices, then add the stock. Bring to the boil and skim off any impurities that rise to the
surface. Reduce the heat and cook the brisket at a slow simmer for 1½ hours, continuing to
skim impurities from the surface and stirring the meat occasionally.

Add the tomatoes, stir and cook for a further 30 minutes, or until the meat is very tender.
Season with sea salt, freshly ground black pepper and lemon juice to taste, and serve
garnished with the coriander leaves.

TRIPE IS ONE OF MY FAVOURITE THINGS. I MIGHT NOT ORDER IT FOR MY LAST MEAL BUT IT IS HIGH ON THE LIST. I THINK TRIPE IS STILL UNDERUTILISED, PERHAPS BECAUSE IT'S PERCEIVED TO BE NOT PARTICULARLY GLAMOROUS, WHICH IS A SHAME AS IT'S INEXPENSIVE AND DELICIOUS.

TRIPE LYONNAISE

4-6 SERVES / MAIN

FOR COOKING THE TRIPE
1 kg (2 lb 4 oz) raw beef honeycomb tripe
1 carrot, roughly chopped
1 onion, roughly chopped
2 celery stalks, roughly chopped
4 garlic cloves, finely chopped
8 thyme sprigs
2 bay leaves
1 tablespoon salt

100 ml (3½ fl oz) olive oil
1.5 kg (3 lb 5 oz) onions, finely sliced
6 garlic cloves, finely chopped
150 ml (5 fl oz) red wine vinegar
2 tablespoons tomato paste (concentrated purée)
1 litre (35 fl oz/4 cups) veal stock
1 large handful of parsley, chopped

Wash the tripe well inside and out under cold running water. Put the carrot, onion and celery in a large saucepan with the tripe, garlic, thyme and bay leaves. Cover with cold water, add the salt and bring to the boil, then reduce the heat and simmer gently for 2–2½ hours, or until the tripe is very tender.

Meanwhile, place a large saucepan over medium heat and add the olive oil. When the oil is hot, add the onions. Caramelise the onions very slowly for about 30 minutes, stirring occasionally to prevent them from sticking to the pan. Add the garlic and cook for 5 minutes, stirring occasionally. Take the pan off the heat and wait until the tripe is cooked.

To check if the tripe is cooked, pierce it with a skewer or a sharp knife; the skewer should pass through easily, with little resistance. Remove the tripe from the pan and allow to cool. Lay the tripe flat on a chopping board, then slice it open and fold it out as you would a book. Now slice the tripe into 5 x 1 cm (2 x ½ inch) pieces and set aside.

Place the vinegar in a medium saucepan and reduce the liquid by half over medium–high heat, then stir in the onions and tomato paste. Add the tripe and stir to combine all the ingredients. Add the stock and bring to a simmer, then reduce the stock slowly by half; it should be slightly sticky. Taste and season with sea salt and freshly ground black pepper, then fold through the parsley. Serve with boiled new potatoes, white beans or a green leaf salad.

WHEN MY DAD WAS YOUNG, ONE OF HIS FAVOURITE MEALS WAS HIS MUM'S RECIPE FOR OX TONGUE. IN THE EARLY YEARS OF MY APPRENTICESHIP I LEARNT TO PREPARE AN OX TONGUE ENTRÉE. WISHING TO SHOW OFF MY NEW-FOUND CULINARY SKILLS, I COOKED, FROZE AND THEN SENT AN OX TONGUE TO HIM. IT TRAVELLED TO BRISBANE IN AN ESKY IN THE LUGGAGE COMPARTMENT OF A BUS.

CHARGRILLED OX TONGUE WITH SALSA VERDE

4 SERVES / STARTER

2 large handfuls of parsley leaves
1 large handful of basil leaves
1 tablespoon salted capers, rinsed
2 garlic cloves
6 anchovy fillets
1 French shallot, cut into quarters
1 thick slice of rustic bread, crust removed and soaked in milk
2 tablespoons white wine vinegar
juice of ½ lemon

125 ml (4 fl oz/½ cup) good-quality olive oil
1 ox tongue
1 carrot, roughly chopped
1 celery stalk, roughly chopped
1 small onion, roughly chopped
6 black peppercorns
1 bay leaf
½ bunch of thyme
olive oil, for frying

To make the salsa verde, put the parsley, basil, capers, garlic, anchovies and shallot into a food processor and pulse until all the ingredients have combined, but there is still some texture to the mixture. Squeeze the excess milk from the bread and add the bread to the mixture along with the vinegar and lemon juice. With the motor running, slowly pour in the olive oil. Taste and adjust the seasoning if necessary, then set aside until needed.

Put the tongue in a saucepan, cover with cold water and bring to the boil. Skim and discard the scum that rises to the surface. Add the carrot, celery, onion, peppercorns, bay leaf, thyme and a pinch of salt. Bring the water back to a simmer and gently cook for 1½ hours. Top up the water occasionally to keep the tongue covered. Check to see if the tongue is cooked by passing a skewer through it; the skewer should meet little resistance. Remove the tongue from the liquid and cool slightly, then peel off the outer skin and remove some of the fatty gristle from the base. Place in a container and refrigerate for 1 hour to firm up.

Remove the tongue from the fridge. Heat a chargrill pan over medium heat until very hot. Slice the tongue into 5 mm (¼ inch) thick pieces. Coat the tongue lightly with olive oil and sear in the hot pan for 1–2 minutes. Arrange on a plate and serve with the salsa verde.

THIS IS A FLAVOURSOME DISH THAT CAN BE MADE UP TO A DAY IN ADVANCE. THIS RECIPE IS FOR FOUR PEOPLE BUT IT'S EASILY MULTIPLIED TO FEED MORE. IF YOU ARE MAKING IT IN ADVANCE, LEAVE THE VEAL IN THE STOCK IN THE FRIDGE, BUT ALLOW IT TO COME TO ROOM TEMPERATURE BEFORE SERVING.

POACHED VEAL LOIN WITH MY TONNATO SAUCE

4 SERVES / MAIN

2 litres (70 fl oz/8 cups) chicken stock
6 garlic cloves, crushed with the back
   of a knife
1 bunch of sage, tied with kitchen string
600 g (1 lb 5 oz) veal loin
1 garlic bulb
2 egg yolks

1 teaspoon dijon mustard
1 tablespoon lemon juice
1 tablespoon white wine vinegar
200 ml (7 fl oz) olive oil
200 g (7 oz) tin of tuna in oil, drained
2 tablespoons salted capers, rinsed
1 small handful of parsley, chopped

Place the stock, garlic cloves and bunch of sage in a large saucepan and bring to the boil. Trim any silver skin from the veal loin. When the stock boils, place the veal into the saucepan. Return the stock to the boil, then reduce the heat to a simmer and cook slowly for 30 minutes (this should achieve medium-rare veal; cook it for a bit longer if you prefer). Remove from the heat and allow the veal to come to room temperature, then remove from the pan.

Preheat the oven to 180°C (350°F/Gas 4). Place the garlic bulb on a baking tray and roast in the oven for 30 minutes, or until the garlic is soft. Allow to cool slightly, then separate and peel the garlic cloves.

To make the tonnato sauce, place the roasted garlic flesh in a food processor with the egg yolks, mustard, lemon juice and vinegar. Pulse the ingredients until they form a smooth paste. With the motor running, slowly pour the olive oil into the food processor until all the ingredients combine into a mayonnaise. Scrape the mayonnaise into a bowl. Put the tuna into the processor's mixing bowl and pulse until the tuna forms a smooth paste. Scrape the tuna paste into a separate bowl, then add half of the roasted garlic mayonnaise and mix well. Now add the remaining mayonnaise and mix until it is well combined. Season to taste with sea salt and freshly ground black pepper. Set aside for later use. (The tonnato sauce can be kept in the fridge for up to 3 days.)

Slice the veal finely and arrange it on a serving platter. Spoon the tonnato sauce over the veal, then scatter over the capers and parsley.

SLOW-COOKED VEAL SHIN WITH TOMATO & HERBS

4-6 SERVES / MAIN

2½ tablespoons olive oil
2 kg (4 lb 8 oz) veal shin, on the bone
3 celery stalks, finely sliced
1½ onions, finely diced
5 garlic cloves, finely chopped
375 ml (13 fl oz/1½ cups) white wine

750 ml (26 fl oz/3 cups) veal stock
750 g (1 lb 10 oz) peeled and chopped
tomatoes (see Note)
1 bunch of basil, picked
½ bunch of parsley, picked
½ bunch of oregano, picked

Place a large flameproof casserole dish over medium–high heat. Add half the olive oil and seal the veal shin in batches on both sides. Remove the shin from the dish and set aside. Wipe the dish clean with paper towel and add the remaining oil. Gently cook the celery, onion and garlic for about 15 minutes until soft.

Return the veal to the dish, stir to combine the ingredients, then pour in the wine and bring to the boil. Reduce the wine by half, then add the stock and return to a simmer. Skim any impurities from the surface, cover and simmer gently for 1 hour. Remove the lid and stir through the tomatoes, then continue to cook gently for 30–45 minutes, or until the meat is very tender.

Season the sauce with sea salt and freshly ground black pepper and stir through the herbs. The herbs add a wonderful freshness to the dish, but if you are planning to freeze some of this dish, do so without adding the herbs.

Note: To peel the tomatoes, score a cross in the base of each tomato. Put the tomatoes in a heatproof bowl and cover with boiling water. Leave for 30–60 seconds, then refresh in a bowl of iced water. Peel the skin away from the cross and discard it, then chop the tomatoes.

PAN-FRIED VEAL LIVER ESCALOPES WITH BACON & CHIVE SAUCE

6 SERVES / MAIN

1 veal (calf) liver (about 1 kg/2 lb 4 oz)
milk, to cover
4 ripe tomatoes
50 g (1¾ oz) butter
2½ tablespoons olive oil
200 g (7 oz) good-quality bacon, cut into
    5 mm (¼ inch) dice
2 garlic cloves, finely chopped

3 French shallots, finely diced
125 ml (4 fl oz/½ cup) white wine
125 ml (4 fl oz/½ cup) chicken stock
125 ml (4 fl oz/½ cup) pouring cream
    (35% fat)
½ teaspoon Tabasco sauce
½ bunch of chives, finely chopped

Clean the membrane from the liver, then slice it into six 1.5 cm (⅝ inch) thick escalopes. Soak the liver escalopes in milk for 30 minutes, then remove them from the milk and dry completely with paper towel.

Meanwhile, to peel the tomatoes, score a cross in the base of each tomato. Put the tomatoes in a heatproof bowl and cover with boiling water. Leave for 30–60 seconds, then refresh in a bowl of iced water. Peel the skin away from the cross and discard it. Cut the tomatoes in half and scoop out the seeds, then cut the flesh into 5 mm (¼ inch) dice.

Heat a large frying pan over medium heat. Depending on the size of your pan you may have to fry the liver in batches. When the pan is hot, add the butter and olive oil. Add the liver and fry for about 2 minutes on each side for medium-rare. Transfer the liver to a plate and leave it in a warm place while you prepare the sauce.

Strain most of the butter and oil from the pan, then add the bacon, garlic and shallots. Fry gently until the bacon crisps slightly and the garlic and shallots start to colour. Add the wine, increase the heat and reduce it by half, then add the stock and reduce the liquid by half again. Add the cream, tomatoes and Tabasco sauce, and reduce the sauce until it thickens slightly. Return the liver to the pan to heat through, and adjust the seasoning with sea salt and freshly ground black pepper. Scatter with the chives before serving.

BROADLY SPEAKING, PEOPLE OF
MY PARENTS' AGE GENERALLY
APPRECIATE VEAL LIVER, BUT
WOULDN'T IT BE FANTASTIC IF
WE ALL GAVE IT A GO.

CONTENTS

DE

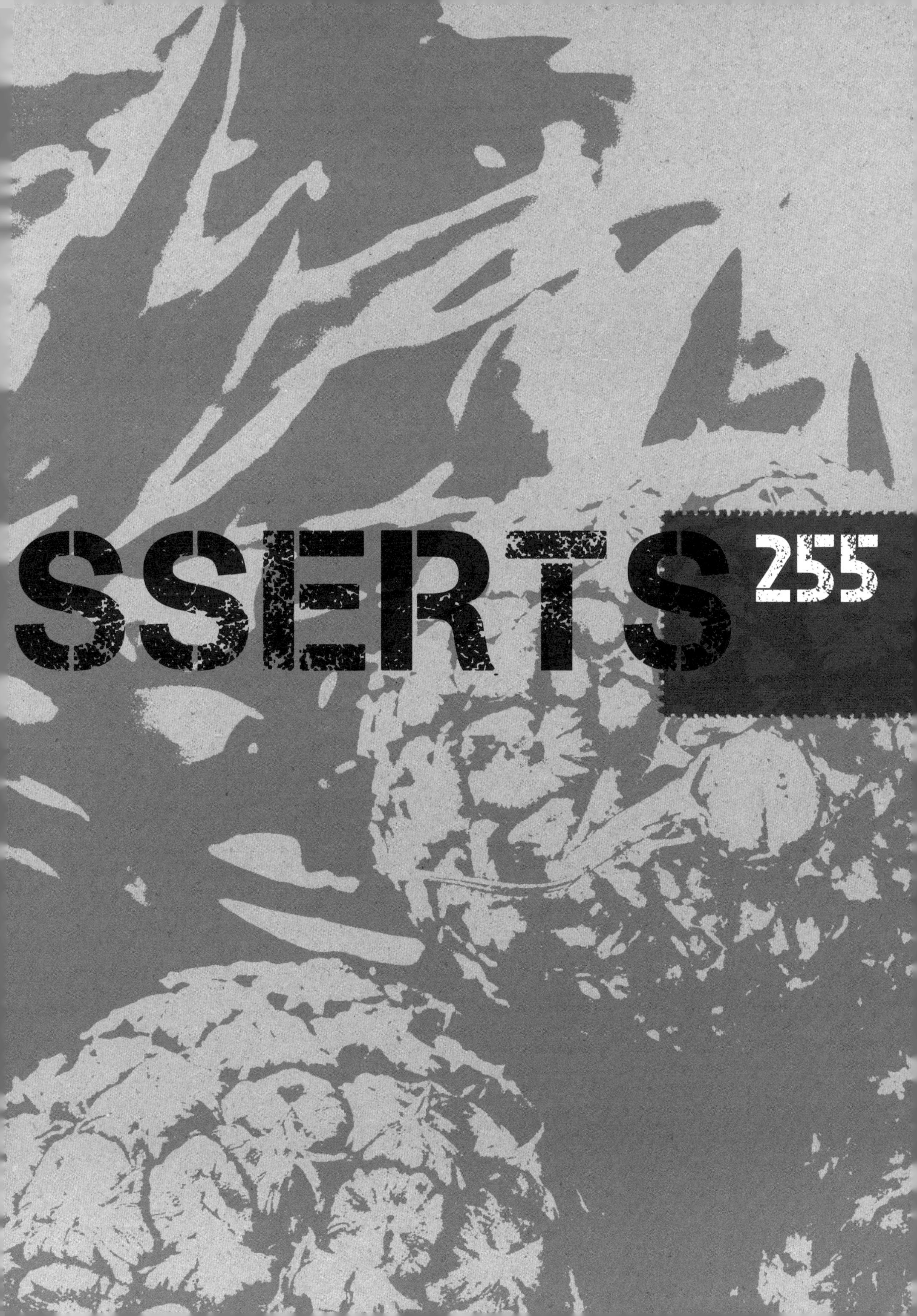
SSERTS
255

DESSERTS

WHEN I THINK OF DESSERT I THINK OF FRENCH CAKES, PASTRIES AND CREAMS. MOST OF THE DESSERTS I HAVE MADE OVER THE COURSE OF MY CAREER HAVE DRAWN INSPIRATION FROM THESE FRENCH CREATIONS. I DIDN'T STUDY TO BE A PASTRY CHEF; MY KITCHEN TRAINING WAS MORE GENERAL, BUT I DID LEARN THE BASICS OF DESSERT PREPARATION.

Small restaurants can't usually afford a professional pastry chef so the person in the kitchen who shows the most interest in making desserts tends to end up with the job. On several occasions, in several different restaurants, that person was yours truly. Over time, through much trial and error, I became quite proficient. When I did eventually work alongside a professional pastry chef though, I realised just how limited my knowledge was. The pastry chef, professionally trained or bestowed by default, is the person who makes the sweet creations for a restaurant's dessert menu. It is a stressful, technically difficult and tiring job. He or she is the first person to start work in the morning and the last to finish at night. In the kitchen, their section is the most organised and could easily be mistaken for a science lab. There are machines for whipping, churning and freezing, drying and extracting. Measuring cups, spoons, jugs, bowls and moulds of all shapes and sizes are artfully arranged on the shelves.

The most important piece of equipment in the kitchen is the oven. When you bake, you need to know your oven intimately. There are always cold and hot spots in conventional ovens. You can easily ruin a cake or choux pastry if you don't know where these spots are. When baking, in my experience, things can and sometimes do go wrong. It is important to learn from your mistakes and not be discouraged. The instructions for dessert recipes are precise and need to be followed, a recipe needs to be read and thoroughly understood before you start, and all the necessary equipment needs to be at hand. I'm not saying this to intimidate you — I'm setting you up for success. A great pastry chef is not born but rather forged through dedication and repeated practice.

Desserts, to a large extent, are seasonal. Rich cakes and puddings are eaten in the cooler months, whereas lighter pastries filled with berries and cream may be preferred in the warmer months. In this chapter I have created a list of desserts utilising a variety of seasonal ingredients and different techniques. Some of the recipes I have used on restaurant menus, others have been inspired by memories of my childhood. Quite often the feature ingredient of a dessert is a fruit. That fruit might only be at its peak and locally available for a short period of time, so many of these recipes can be adapted, substituting whatever fruit is in season.

Finally, it is my sincere hope that the skills you gain while preparing these desserts will give you the confidence to approach any dessert recipe in the future with gusto.

MUM HAS BEEN EFFORTLESSLY MAKING THESE SENSATIONAL CREAM PUFFS FOR AS LONG AS I CAN REMEMBER. CREAM PUFFS, OR CHOUX BUNS AS THEY ARE CLASSICALLY KNOWN, HAVE BECOME THE CULINARY CHALLENGE DU JOUR. THE RECIPE IS A LITTLE TECHNICAL BUT DON'T BE DISCOURAGED; ALL GOOD THINGS COME TO THOSE WHO PRACTISE. GIVEN TIME, YOU MAY BECOME CONFIDENT ENOUGH TO TACKLE YOUR VERY OWN CROQUEMBOUCHE.

CREAM PUFFS WITH CHANTILLY CREAM

25 PUFFS

100 g (3½ oz) unsalted butter
a pinch of salt
a pinch of sugar
125 g (4½ oz) plain (all-purpose) flour, sifted
4 eggs
icing (confectioners') sugar, for dusting

CHANTILLY CREAM
½ vanilla bean or ½ teaspoon natural vanilla extract
200 ml (7 fl oz) pouring cream (35% fat)
1 tablespoon icing (confectioners') sugar, sifted

Put 250 ml (9 fl oz/1 cup) of water and the butter in a saucepan and bring to the boil. Stir in the salt and sugar, then remove the saucepan from the heat. Add the flour and stir vigorously with a wooden spoon until the mixture forms a loose dough. Return the saucepan to the stovetop over medium heat and constantly stir the dough until it comes away from the side of the pan. Remove the pan from the heat and allow the mixture to cool for 5 minutes.

Crack and add the eggs to the dough one at a time, stirring to incorporate completely before adding the next egg. When all of the eggs have been added to the mixture it should be moist, and when lifted out of the saucepan with a spoon it should be elastic and want to drop slowly off the spoon back into the saucepan.

Preheat the oven to 220°C (425°F/Gas 7). Line two baking trays with baking paper. Place a good tablespoonful of the dough on the baking paper, leaving a 4 cm (1½ inch) space between each. Continue in this way until you have used all the dough. Bake for 10–15 minutes, or until the dough has risen and is a nice golden colour. Remove the puffs from the oven and allow them to cool completely.

Meanwhile, make the chantilly cream. If you are using the vanilla bean, split it lengthways and scrape out the seeds. Add the seeds (or vanilla extract) to a bowl with the cream and icing sugar and whisk together until stiff. Cut a small incision in the top of the puffs, carefully open them up with your fingers and fill with the cream. Dust with icing sugar before serving.

I OWE A GREAT DEAL OF GRATITUDE TO THIS RECIPE. IT'S EASY TO MAKE, CAN BE USED IN A VARIETY OF WAYS, AND IT ALWAYS SOLD WELL WHEN ON MY DESSERT MENU. IT IS A DELICIOUSLY MOIST CAKE AND THE RECIPE IS EASILY MULTIPLIED TO CATER FOR A CROWD.

CHOCOLATE ROULADE WITH HAZELNUT CREAM

8 SERVES

125 g (4½ oz) unsalted butter, cubed
100 g (3½ oz) dark chocolate (64%), chopped
220 g (7¾ oz/1 cup) caster (superfine) sugar
125 ml (4 fl oz/½ cup) hot water
2 tablespoons scotch whisky
3 teaspoons espresso coffee
30 g (1 oz/¼ cup) unsweetened cocoa powder, plus extra, for dusting
35 g (1¼ oz/¼ cup) plain (all-purpose) flour
75 g (2½ oz/½ cup) self-raising flour
1 egg, lightly beaten

FRANGELICO SUGAR SYRUP
55 g (2 oz/¼ cup) caster (superfine) sugar
1½ tablespoons Frangelico liqueur

HAZELNUT CREAM
85 g (3 oz) unsalted butter, room temperature
85 g (3 oz/⅔ cup) icing (confectioners') sugar, sifted
85 g (3 oz) toasted hazelnuts, crushed

To make the Frangelico sugar syrup, combine the sugar and 3 tablespoons of water in a small saucepan. Bring to the boil over medium heat, stirring constantly until the sugar dissolves. Remove from the heat, add the Frangelico and set aside to cool.

To make the hazelnut cream, cream the butter and icing sugar until it is light and fluffy. Gently stir the hazelnuts through the mixture and set aside.

Preheat the oven to 150°C (300°F/Gas 2). Put the butter, chocolate, sugar, hot water, whisky and coffee in a heatproof bowl and set the bowl over a saucepan of simmering water. When the butter and chocolate melt, stir the ingredients with a plastic or metal spoon to dissolve the sugar. Remove the bowl from the pan and stir through the cocoa powder and both flours. This will be lumpy, so use a hand whisk to whisk the mixture until smooth. Cool slightly, then stir through the egg.

Grease and line a shallow 32 x 25 cm (12¾ x 10 inch) baking tray with non-stick baking paper. Pour the cake mixture into the tray — it should be about 1 cm (½ inch) thick. Bake for 10–12 minutes. To check if the cake is done, insert a skewer into the cake; it is cooked if the skewer comes out clean, and the top of the cake is springy to touch.

Remove from the oven and cool for 5 minutes, turn out onto a wire rack and carefully peel away the baking paper. Lay a kitchen cloth over the cake and allow it to cool slightly, then carefully turn the cake over so it is sitting on top of the cloth. Brush a liberal amount of the Frangelico sugar syrup over the cake, then spread a layer of hazelnut cream over the top, leaving a 2.5 cm (1 inch) border on one of the longest sides. With the other longest side of the cloth facing you, pick up the two corners and, using the cloth to assist you, roll the cake up into a roulade. Place in the fridge for 1 hour to set. Bring to room temperature for 30 minutes before serving. Dust with cocoa powder and serve with berries.

AGAR AGAR IS A GELATINOUS SUBSTANCE EXTRACTED FROM SEAWEED; IT IS THE VEGETARIAN'S GELATINE. I THINK IT IS MORE PRACTICAL THAN GELATINE BECAUSE IT SETS LIQUID WITHOUT REFRIGERATION. THIS MEANS THE JELLIES ARE QUITE PORTABLE, PERFECT FOR PICNICS OR FOR WHENEVER YOU WANT A HEALTHY FRUIT-FLAVOURED TREAT. YOU CAN BUY AGAR AGAR FROM ASIAN GROCERY STORES.

ASIAN FRUIT SALAD WITH AGAR AGAR JELLIES & COCONUT CREAM

4 SERVES

500 ml (17 fl oz/2 cups) watermelon juice
500 ml (17 fl oz/2 cups) pineapple juice
12 g (½ oz) agar agar powder
2 tablespoons sugar
juice of ½ lemon
16 lychees, peeled and pitted
3 mangosteens

3 passionfruit
1 mango
1 quantity coconut cream (page 269)
2 tablespoons crushed toasted peanuts (see Note)

Place the watermelon juice and the pineapple juice in separate saucepans. Stir 5 g (⅛ oz) of agar agar into the watermelon juice and 7 g (¼ oz) into the pineapple juice. Add 125 ml (4 fl oz/½ cup) of water, 1 tablespoon of sugar and the lemon juice to the watermelon juice. Add 125 ml (4 fl oz/½ cup) of water and 1 tablespoon of sugar to the pineapple juice. Place the saucepans over high heat and bring to the boil, stirring constantly. Once the juices boil, remove the pans from the heat.

Strain both the watermelon juice and pineapple juice through muslin cloth into separate, square heatproof containers. Allow the jelly to cool at room temperature. Once the jellies have set, cut them into 1 cm (½ inch) square or diamond shapes, then lift them out of the container and place them in the fridge.

Meanwhile, prepare the fruit for the salad, then arrange it in serving bowls. Scatter over the jelly squares and pour the coconut cream over the top. Garnish with the toasted peanuts.

Note: To toast the peanuts, put 3 tablespoons of raw peanuts on a microwave-safe plate. Cook for 2 minutes on high. Allow the nuts to cool, then crush using a mortar and pestle. This will give about 2 tablespoons of crushed peanuts.

AGAR AGAR HAS STRONGER SETTING
PROPERTIES THAN GELATINE,
ALTHOUGH ITS GELLING ABILITY
DEPENDS ON WHAT IT'S BEING USED TO
SET. MORE ACIDIC FRUITS AND FRUIT
JUICES, SUCH AS STRAWBERRY OR
CITRUS, MAY NEED GREATER AMOUNTS.

MY CHOCOLATE MOUSSE IS A GOOD ALL-ROUNDER. IT CAN BE EATEN
ON ITS OWN WITH BERRIES AND BISCUITS, USED TO TOP OR FILL
A CAKE, OR TO ACCOMPANY OR FILL THE CHOCOLATE ROULADE
(PAGE 263). WHEN YOU MAKE IT, USE 'LIGHT' HANDS, AS YOU WANT
THE FINAL MOUSSE TO BE AS LIGHT AS POSSIBLE.

MY SIMPLE YET DECADENT CHOCOLATE MOUSSE

6–8 SERVES

225 g (8 oz) dark chocolate (64%), chopped
3 tablespoons Cointreau
90 g (3¼ oz) unsalted butter, at room
   temperature, cut into small pieces

6 eggs, separated
75 g (2½ oz/⅓ cup) caster (superfine)
   sugar

Half fill a large saucepan with water, place it over high heat and bring to a simmer. Place the chocolate and Cointreau in a heatproof bowl and set the bowl over the pan of water, ensuring the base of the bowl isn't touching the water. Melt the chocolate, stirring occasionally, then remove the bowl from the heat and stir through the butter.

Beat the egg whites in a clean, dry bowl until they are stiff but not dry. Whisk the egg yolks and sugar together until the mixture is light and fluffy, then stir it through the chocolate. Add half of the beaten egg whites to the chocolate mixture — use a spatula or large kitchen spoon in a gentle circular mixing motion to incorporate the egg whites. Fold this mixture back through the remaining egg whites.

Spoon the chocolate mousse into individual moulds or one large mould and refrigerate for 2 hours. Allow the mousse to sit at room temperature for 20 minutes before serving.

A CLAFOUTIS IS LIKE A BIG GLORIOUS PANCAKE. A DECADENTLY
RICH BATTER COVERS THE MACERATED CHERRIES, WHICH IS THEN
BAKED UNTIL GOLDEN. IT IS VERY FRENCH AND VERY DELICIOUS.

CLAFOUTIS

6 SERVES

750 g (1 lb 10 oz) cherries, pitted
125 ml (4 fl oz/½ cup) Kirsch
20 g (¾ oz) unsalted butter, softened
45 g (1½ oz/¼ cup) soft brown sugar
6 eggs
115 g (4 oz/½ cup) caster (superfine) sugar

35 g (1¼ oz/¼ cup) plain (all-purpose)
   flour, sifted
125 g (4½ oz/½ cup) thick (double/heavy)
   cream (45% fat or above)
a pinch of salt

Marinate the cherries in a bowl with the Kirsch for 1 hour. Use the butter to grease a 25 cm
(10 inch) square, 7 cm (2¾ inch) deep baking dish or a deep 30 cm (12 inch) ovenproof cast-
iron frying pan. Sprinkle the brown sugar evenly over the base of the dish.

Preheat the oven to 200°C (400°F/Gas 6). Place the eggs and sugar in the bowl of an
electric mixer and mix at high speed until the mixture is light and fluffy. Lower the speed,
then add the flour, cream and salt; the mixture will be of a batter consistency. Drain the liquid
from the cherries and pour it slowly into the batter mixture, then stir to combine.

Arrange the cherries across the base of the baking dish, then cover them with the batter.
Bake for 25 minutes, or until the top of the clafoutis is golden brown and bounces back when
touched. Remove from the oven and allow to cool slightly before serving.

COCONUT- & RICE-COATED BANANA FRITTERS WITH COCONUT CREAM

4 SERVES

BANANA FRITTERS

95 g (3¼ oz/½ cup) cooked jasmine rice,
    left to dry in the fridge overnight
45 g (1½ oz/½ cup) desiccated coconut
4 cavendish bananas
plain (all-purpose) flour, for dusting
1 egg, lightly beaten
2 litres (70 fl oz/8 cups) vegetable oil,
    for deep-frying

COCONUT CREAM

400 ml (14 fl oz) coconut cream
1 tablespoon caster (superfine) sugar
½ teaspoon salt
2 teaspoons potato starch

PALM SUGAR CARAMEL

45 g (1½ oz/⅓ cup) grated palm sugar
    (jaggery)

To make the coconut cream, put the coconut cream, sugar, salt and potato starch in
a saucepan and mix well. Place the saucepan over medium heat and stir the mixture for
3–4 minutes until it starts to thicken. Remove from the heat and set aside to cool.

To make the banana fritters, rub the cooked rice and coconut together in a bowl with your
hands. Peel the bananas, then cut them in half lengthways on the diagonal. Lightly dust the
banana pieces in the flour, roll them through the beaten egg, then coat them with the rice
and coconut mixture. You may need to press the mixture into the flesh of the banana a little.

Heat the oil in a large heavy-based saucepan or deep-fryer to 180°C (350°F), or until a cube
of bread dropped into the oil turns golden brown in 15 seconds. When the oil is hot, fry the
bananas, a couple at a time, until golden brown. Remove and drain on paper towel.

To make the palm sugar caramel, put the palm sugar in a small heavy-based saucepan with
2 tablespoons of water. Place over medium–high heat and cook, shaking the pan occasionally
to ensure even cooking. When the sugar is dark golden and caramelised, remove the pan
from the heat.

Pour some coconut cream into each bowl, top with banana fritters and drizzle with the
palm sugar caramel.

MILK IS MILK, RIGHT?

ONCE IT WAS THAT SIMPLE. NOW MILK IS 2 PER CENT FAT, LOW FAT, NO FAT WITH ADDED CALCIUM AND PROBIOTICS. MILK TODAY IS DECONSTRUCTED IN THE DAIRY, THEN REFORMULATED DEPENDING ON THE MARKETING REQUIREMENT. FAT'S BAD? NO, IT'S GOOD! WELL IT'S BAD TODAY, GOOD TOMORROW AND IN THE FUTURE WE'LL BUY WHATEVER THE MARKETING GURUS DECIDE IS GOOD FOR US.

Believe it or not, milk is a seasonal product and its flavour and fat content changes throughout the year, influenced by the quantity and quality of the grass the cattle eat. Milk is now engineered to prevent this — to maintain a consistent flavour at all times. We are becoming more and more removed from food in its natural, raw state.

Growing up we would drink milk straight from my uncle's Jersey cow, Sadie. Sadie kept the grass in order and produced abundant, rich full-fat milk. We'd put Sadie's milk in the fridge and within an hour there would be a thick solid mass of glorious cream floating on the top. It was milk in its natural raw state — from the udder to the table. The experience of drinking raw milk may be lost forever unless you are fortunate enough to own a cow or know someone who does (but remember the sale of raw milk is currently illegal in Australia, and any farmers caught selling it may be fined).

The majority of Australia's dairy farms are family owned and operated, with a herd size ranging between 85 and 200 head of cattle. Although the Jersey cow is a sentimental favourite, the most popular breed of dairy cow today is the Holstein Friesian. These cows are preferred because their milk production is far greater than a Jersey's, although many people, like myself, believe the milk is of an inferior quality.

Over the last two decades, by utilising better pasture management, selective breeding and feed supplements, the industry has managed to almost double the average annual yield per cow from 2850 litres to over 5000 litres. This quantity of milk is far greater than a cow would naturally produce to feed a calf. Cows can live for 20 years, although cattle in a modern dairy seldom live beyond seven. This decline in health is a result of the stress of the increased milk production. The cattle can become lame from walking great distances over uneven ground to the milking sheds, carrying the enormous weight of their engorged udders. The udders themselves can become infected; clinical mastitis is estimated to affect 5 per cent of the national dairy herd. There are other welfare issues, some of which I have covered in the Beef and Veal chapter (page 223), as the two industries are directly linked. Dairy cattle, like all other animals domesticated for our benefit, have their physical limitations. Codes of practice exist for their welfare. It is up to us as consumers to be vigilant and ensure these are upheld.

My family and I enjoy full-cream milk bought from an independent producer. The sad thing is that most children will grow up without ever experiencing the simple pleasure of a real full-cream milk moustache.

PEAR & FRANGIPANE TART

8 SERVES

750 g (1 lb 10 oz) sugar
1 cinnamon stick
6 black peppercorns
rind of ½ lemon
2 packham pears

PASTRY
225 g (8 oz/1½ cups) plain (all-purpose)
   flour
160 g (5½ oz) salted butter, cut into
   1 cm (½ inch) cubes, at room
   temperature for 30 minutes
2 tablespoons icing (confectioners') sugar

1 egg yolk
1 tablespoon cold milk

FRANGIPANE
125 g (4½ oz) unsalted butter, cubed,
   at room temperature
125 g (4½ oz/1 cup) icing (confectioners')
   sugar
125 g (4½ oz/1¼ cups) ground almonds
25 g (1 oz) plain (all-purpose) flour
2 eggs
1 tablespoon rum

Combine the sugar and 750 ml (26 fl oz/3 cups) of water in a saucepan, then place the pan over high heat, stirring until the sugar dissolves. Add the cinnamon, peppercorns and lemon rind and bring to the boil. Remove from the heat and allow the sugar syrup to cool slightly. Meanwhile peel and core the pears. Place the pears in the syrup, cover with a piece of baking paper and simmer gently until the pears are tender but still holding their shape. This will take anywhere between 35 minutes and 1 hour, depending on the ripeness of the pears. Once cooked, leave to cool in the syrup, then slice lengthways into 2 cm (¾ inch) wedges.

While the pears are cooking, make the pastry for the tart shell. Put the flour on a work surface. Put the butter and icing sugar on top and work together with your fingertips. Make a well in the flour mixture, add the egg yolk, then gradually start to work in the yolk until it is almost completely combined. To finish the dough, incorporate the milk, then knead the dough gently for 30 seconds. Cover in plastic wrap and put in the fridge to rest for 1 hour.

To make the frangipane, cream the butter and icing sugar in an electric mixer at medium speed. Turn the mixer off and add the ground almonds, flour, eggs and rum. Mix at slow speed to combine, then reserve for later use.

Remove the dough from the fridge and allow it to come to room temperature. Roll out on a lightly floured surface or between two sheets of non-stick baking paper to a 2.5 mm (¹⁄₁₆ inch) thickness and use it to line a 22 cm (8½ inch) loose-based tart tin. Trim, then gently prick the base with a fork. Refrigerate for 30 minutes. Preheat the oven to 180°C (350°F/Gas 4).

Line the base of the tart shell with a piece of baking paper, weigh it down with some baking beads or rice and blind bake the shell for 10 minutes, or until the sides are just golden. Remove the baking paper and beads and return to the oven for a further 5–10 minutes until the base is light golden. Cover the base with the frangipane, then decoratively arrange the pear wedges on top. Return the tart to the oven and bake for 20–25 minutes, or until the frangipane has set. Allow the tart to cool and serve with thick cream or clotted cream.

FRANGIPANE COMPLEMENTS ALL FRUIT, SO BE CREATIVE AND LET THE SEASON BE YOUR GUIDE. USE FRUIT AT THE PEAK OF THE SEASON, SUCH AS PEACHES AND CARAMELISED PINEAPPLE IN SUMMER, AND APPLES AND PEARS IN WINTER.

274

IT WOULDN'T BE CHRISTMAS FOR THE JENSEN FAMILY WITHOUT MY MUM'S STEAMED PUDDING, WHICH USES ONE OF HER FAVOURITE TREATS, GLACÉ GINGER.

STEAMED GINGER PUDDING

6 SERVES

90 g (3¼ oz) unsalted butter, at room temperature
2 teaspoons finely grated orange zest
60 g (2¼ oz/⅓ cup) soft brown sugar
75 g (2½ oz/¼ cup) candied honey (creamed honey)
2 eggs
2 tablespoons chopped glacé ginger
150 g (5½ oz/1 cup) self-raising flour, sifted

1 teaspoon ground ginger
125 ml (4 fl oz/½ cup) milk

GINGER CREAM SAUCE
500 ml (17 fl oz/2 cups) ginger wine
45 g (1½ oz/¼ cup) soft brown sugar
125 g (4½ oz/½ cup) thick (double/heavy) cream (45% fat or above)
a pinch of salt

Beat the butter, orange zest, brown sugar and candied honey together in an electric mixer until light and fluffy. Reduce the speed to slow, then add the eggs, glacé ginger, flour and ground ginger. When the mixture has come together, slowly add the milk in two batches.

Grease and flour six 170 ml (5½ fl oz/⅔ cup) pudding moulds, then divide the mixture among the moulds. Cover the tops of the puddings with greased rounds of non-stick baking paper (cut to fit) and place in a steamer set over high heat. Steam for 15–20 minutes, or until the puddings are cooked through when tested with a skewer. Remove the baking paper and carefully remove the puddings from the moulds.

While the puddings are cooking, make the ginger cream sauce. Pour the ginger wine into a saucepan and reduce by half over high heat. Add the brown sugar, cream and salt and bring to the boil. Reduce the heat immediately and reduce the sauce until it thickens slightly.

Place a ginger pudding in the centre of each serving bowl. Pour the ginger cream sauce over the pudding and serve with whipped cream or ice cream.

MINI SAVARIN CAKES WITH POACHED KUMQUATS

60 MINI SAVARIN CAKES

POACHED KUMQUATS & RUM SYRUP
500 g (1 lb 2 oz) kumquats
330 g (11½ oz/1½ cups) sugar
125 ml (4 fl oz/½ cup) dark rum

SAVARIN CAKES
250 g (9 oz/1⅔ cups) plain (all-purpose) flour
100 ml (3½ fl oz) warm milk

7 g (¼ oz/1 sachet) dried yeast
2 eggs
75 g (2½ oz) unsalted butter, cut into 1 cm (½ inch) cubes, at room temperature, plus extra butter, for greasing
1½ teaspoons caster (superfine) sugar
1 teaspoon salt

chantilly cream (page 260), to serve

To poach the kumquats and make the rum syrup, pierce all the kumquats with a fork and set aside. Combine the sugar and 750 ml (26 fl oz/3 cups) of water in a saucepan. Place the saucepan over high heat, stir to dissolve the sugar, and bring to the boil. Add the kumquats and gently simmer for 40 minutes, then remove from the heat and allow to cool. To make the rum syrup, strain off 500 ml (17 fl oz/2 cups) of the poaching liquid and stir through the rum. Set the poached kumquats and the rum syrup aside.

To make the savarin cakes, sift the flour into a large bowl and make a well in the centre. Add half the warm milk and all of the yeast to the well and mix with a fork to combine. Position the bowl in a warm place for 10 minutes to allow the yeast to ferment or bubble, then add the remaining milk and the eggs to the well. Using your hands, start to incorporate the ingredients, then tip the dough out of the bowl onto a lightly floured surface (it is quite a sticky dough) and knead together gently until it just comes together in a silky textured ball. Return the dough to the bowl and dot it with the butter cubes. Place a damp kitchen cloth over the top and allow the dough to prove until it is not quite double in size, then add the sugar and salt and knead to combine.

Preheat the oven to 200°C (400°F/Gas 6). Grease two 20-hole madeleine cake tins (4.5 x 3 cm/1¾ x 1¼ inches wide) and fill each with a heaped teaspoon of dough. Leave the tins in a warm place for about 10 minutes, or until the dough rises once more. Place the tins in the oven and bake for 5–7 minutes, or until a skewer inserted into the centre of a cake comes out clean. Repeat for the remaining mixture.

Remove the savarin cakes from the oven and allow to cool slightly. Warm the reserved rum syrup and soak the cakes in the syrup. Serve with the poached kumquats and chantilly cream.

IT TAKES A BIT OF PRACTICE TO
MASTER THE ART OF BAKING YEASTED
PRODUCTS, BUT THIS RECIPE IS A GOOD
PLACE TO START. IF THE CAKES DON'T
TURN OUT QUITE RIGHT THE FIRST
TIME, I GUARANTEE YOU WILL STILL
HAVE A PRESENTABLE PRODUCT. ONCE
SOAKED IN THE SYRUP, ANY FLAWS
WILL BE UNNOTICEABLE.

APPLE AND PECAN PIE REMINDS ME
OF SUNDAYS WITH MY FAMILY AS
A CHILD, WHEN WE WOULD HAVE
THIS AFTER OUR TRADITIONAL
BAKED DINNER. THIS RECIPE HOLDS
A SPECIAL PLACE IN OUR FAMILY'S
CULINARY ARCHIVE.

APPLE & PECAN PIE

8 SERVES

6 granny smith or golden delicious apples
grated zest and juice of 1 lemon
200 g (7 oz) soft brown sugar
100 g (3½ oz) unsalted butter
100 g (3½ oz/1 cup) pecans
2 teaspoons cornflour (cornstarch)
1 egg, lightly beaten with 1 tablespoon milk

PASTRY
500 g (1 lb 2 oz/3⅓ cups) plain
  (all-purpose) flour
160 g (5½ oz) unsalted butter, cut into 5 mm
  (¼ inch) cubes, at room temperature
60 g (2¼ oz/½ cup) icing (confectioners')
  sugar
2 egg yolks, lightly beaten
2 tablespoons cold milk

To make the pastry, put the flour on a work surface. Put the butter and icing sugar on top and work the ingredients together with your fingertips. Make a well in the flour mixture, add the egg yolk, then gradually work in the yolk until they are almost completely combined. To finish the dough, incorporate the milk, then knead the dough gently for 30 seconds. Cover in plastic wrap and put in the fridge to rest for 1 hour.

Roll out two-thirds of the pastry on a lightly floured surface or between two sheets of non-stick baking paper to a 3–4 mm (⅛ inch) thickness. Line a 4.5 cm (1¾ inch) deep, 22 cm (8½ inch) pie dish with the pastry and prick the base with a fork. Similarly, roll out the remaining pastry to a 5 mm (¼ inch) thickness (for the lattice top), and place on a tray. Refrigerate both the pastry-lined dish and the pastry for the lattice top for 30 minutes.

Peel, quarter and core the apples. Place the apple quarters into a bowl with the lemon zest, juice and brown sugar. Mix to combine the ingredients and set aside for 15 minutes. Preheat the oven to 180°C (350°F/Gas 4).

Place a frying pan over medium heat and add the butter. When the butter starts to bubble, add the pecans and cook for 2 minutes. Add the apple mixture and gently sauté for 5 minutes. Remove the pan from the heat, carefully remove the apples and pecans with a slotted spoon and place them in a bowl. Return the pan to the heat, add the cornflour and cook out the brown sugar sauce for 2–3 minutes, or until reduced and thickened. Pour the sauce over the apples and pecans and leave to cool at room temperature.

Remove the pie dish from the fridge. Line the base with a piece of baking paper, weigh it down with some baking beads or rice and blind bake for 15 minutes until just golden. Remove the paper and beads and cool slightly. Brush the pie base with the egg wash, return to the oven for 2–3 minutes, then remove from the oven and set aside to cool completely.

Remove the pastry for the lattice from the fridge and allow it to sit at room temperature for 2 minutes. Cut the pastry into 1 cm (½ inch) wide strips. Fill the pie base with the cooled apple filling. Brush the egg wash around the edge of the pie, then weave the pastry strips vertically and horizontally across the top of the pie. Crimp to secure the lattice to the edge of the pie and trim the edges. Brush the egg wash over the top of the lattice strips, then bake for 30 minutes. Serve with vanilla ice cream.

INDEX

BIBLIOGRAPHY

Clover, C, *The End of the Line: How Overfishing is Changing the World and What We Eat*, Ebury Press, London, 2005.

Crocombe, A, *Ethical Eating*, Penguin Books, Australia, 2008.

Evans, M, *The Real Food Companion*, Murdoch Books, Sydney, 2010.

Fearnley-Whittingstall, H (foreward) & Soil Association, *Home Grown: A Practical Guide to Self-Sufficiency and Living the Good Life*, Gaia, a division of Octopus Publishing Group Limited, London, 2009.

Fearnley-Whittingstall, H, *The River Cottage Meat Book*, Hodder & Stoughton, London, 2004.

Flannery, T, 'Now or Never: A Sustainable Future for Australia?', Quarterly Essay No 38, Black Inc., Collingwood, Victoria, 2008.

Pollan, M, *In Defense of Food*, The Penguin Press, New York, 2008.

Singer, P & Mason J, *The Ethics of What We Eat*, Text Publishing, Melbourne, 2006.

Stokes, C & Howard, M, *Adapting Agriculture to Climate Change*, CSIRO Publishing, Victoria, 2010.

WEBSITES

www.australianpork.com.au
www.chicken.org.au
www.climatechange.gov.au
www.csiro.au
www.environment.gov.au
www.mla.com.au
www.montereybayaquarium.org
www.rbta.org/pigs.htm
www.theecologist.org

First published in 2011 by Murdoch Books Pty Limited

Murdoch Books Australia
Pier 8/9
23 Hickson Road
Millers Point NSW 2000
Phone: +61 (0) 2 8220 2000
Fax: +61 (0) 2 8220 2558
www.murdochbooks.com.au

Murdoch Books UK Limited
Erico House, 6th Floor
93–99 Upper Richmond Road
Putney, London SW15 2TG
Phone: +44 (0) 20 8785 5995
Fax: +44 (0) 20 8785 5985
www.murdochbooks.co.uk

Publisher: Kylie Walker
Concept and design: Reuben Crossman
Photographer: Cath Muscat
Stylist: Michelle Noerianto
Food preparation: Andrew de Sousa
Editor: Kim Rowney
Food editor: Sonia Greig
Production: Alexandra Gonzalez

National Library of Australia Cataloguing-in-
Publication entry

Author: Jensen, Mark, 1967-.
Title: The urban cook: cooking and
                 eating for a sustainable future /
                 Mark Jensen.
ISBN: 9781741967234 (hbk.)
Notes: Includes index.
Subjects: Cooking
                 Seasonal cooking
                 Sustainable living
Dewey Number: 641.564

A catalogue record for this book is available from
the British Library.

Colour separation by Splitting Image Colour Studio,
Melbourne, Australia.

The publisher and photographer wish to thank
Moss Vale High School; Pasquale Multari and Cindy
Bowman from Tre Porcellini farm in Moss Vale; and
Victor Churchill Butchers, Woollahra. Thank you
also to Cambodia House and Major & Tom for their
generosity in supplying props for photography.

IMPORTANT: Those who might be at risk from the
effects of salmonella poisoning (the elderly, pregnant
women, young children and those suffering from
immune deficiency diseases) should consult their
doctor with any concerns about eating raw eggs.

OVEN GUIDE: You may find cooking times vary
depending on the oven you are using. We have used
a fan-forced oven for these recipes. As a general rule,
increase the oven temperature by 20°C (35°F) if using
a conventional oven.

Printed by 1010 Printing International Ltd in 2011.
PRINTED IN CHINA.

FSC

Mixed Sources
Product group from well-managed
forests and other controlled sources
www.fsc.org Cert no SGS-COC-004334
© 1996 Forest Stewardship Council

BUY THIS MUST HA

CHEAP NOW TO WORK

BIG SCREE

SEASONAL PRODUCE MUS

MY LIFE THE

BIG SCREEN

CLIMATE CHANGE BE

SUSTAINABILITY FOOTPRI

ETHICS CONVENTI

BIODYNAM

KILOJOULES CALORIES

CARBON FOOTPRINT

AKE UPGRA

RESPONSIBILITY CI

MORTGAGE VALUE CI

WATER FOOTPRI

ENJOY LIFE EAT

EXERCISE MORE

LEGACY FAST